ROAD TRIP
TO
REDEMPTION

ROAD TRIP
TO
REDEMPTION

Living in Darkness and Finding My Way Out

CHRISTOPHER D CRAIG SR

XULON PRESS

Xulon Press
2301 Lucien Way #415
Maitland, FL 32751
407.339.4217
www.xulonpress.com

Paperback ISBN-13: 978-1-66286-576-3

Ebook ISBN-13: 978-1-66286-577-0

If the old sayings, "What does not kill us makes us stronger" and "This is the first day of the rest of your life" are true, then first, I am surprised to still be here to author this book, and second, I am very blessed to still be here to author this book. I started out as an overweight under-achiever who only wanted to be noticed, then became a self-centered, egotistical hoax who only did what he wanted and only made time for self-gratification, followed by someone who was a religiously lost, broken toy. Finally, after hitting rock-bottom, I realized who I really was: a follower of the Son of God, who is the "One True King" and My Lord and Savior, Jesus Christ.

How would you like to go an adventure with me? It is a walk, really; not a straight path, but one with many turns, trials, and tribulations. Just remember that no matter the depth of the hole that you are in, all anyone must do is start by looking up.

Psalms 40:2, NIV

He lifted me out of the pit, out of the mud and mire; He set my feet on a rock and gave me a firm place to stand.

This book is dedicated to the following, with love and respect:

Jesus Christ, for being the hand that guides me
Beth Ann, my beautiful wife and confidant
Katie and Jacob, who make my life complete
Jersey, Lilli, and Marley, forever faithful
The Craig and McMillion Families
Tommy, Jon, and Kelly
Pastor Shawn, Chuck, Ellery, and Dan
Tom and Melinda
Pastor Scott and Matt
and the Blue Ridge Church Family
All of our military, veterans, and first responders

CHAPTER 1

My earliest memories were of living in a neighborhood called "Davey Gardens," which was located on the south side of the city of Richmond, the state capital of Virginia. It was a typical middle-class area, with lots of hard-working families and lots of kids to play with. I was the fifth of six children, born into a Scotch-Irish/Italian Roman Catholic family. Our mother, Frances Ann, was a first-generation Italian American from Massachusetts, and my pop, Charles Lee Craig, Sr., was of Scotch/Irish descent. They met in Massachusetts when he was in the Army. There are three girls and three boys in our family. They are, in order of birth: Cynthia; Sharon; Charles, Jr. (Charlie/Boo); Michael; me; and Laura. My older sisters graduated from catholic school; my two older brothers went through the eighth grade and then switched over to public school. I grew up going to catholic school until fourth grade, and my younger sister only attended public school. Our parents made sure that we had what we needed, but with six kids, times were tight, to say the least. We all grew up going to Buckroe Beach in Hampton, Virginia every summer. It was a family affair. We would get an efficiency hotel room with our grandparents, Pop's parents. Pop's aunts and uncles, including cousins, would all be staying at the same motel. It was called the Sans Souci. Granny and Paw-Paw Craig had been going there ever since they were young. It was great, in those days. The fishing pier was a short walk from the motel, and there was an amusement park next-door. I rode my first roller coaster there. It was called "The Dips." We went there until around the mid-eighties.

To help Pop out, Mom was always babysitting lots of kids, so she could stay at home with us, especially Charlie. He was born with Spina Bifida and would either use braces and crutches or a wheelchair. Mom nicknamed him "Boo," because she said that he reminded her of Boo-Boo Bear, Yogi's sidekick; so, that is what we would call him. Some of the kids she baby-sat were family, friends of the family, and/or neighborhood kids. Kids were always drawn to our house, even when we had moved to the next one. Dad, or "Pop," as I would later call him and will refer to him from here on out, worked swing shifts in the extrusion department, for what was then called Reynolds Metals. Just like his father did. Both would eventually retire from there. He also picked up shifts at a hardware store to help make ends meet.

I was the typical catholic kid, however. I was a *big dreamer*, and that was not something that tow-the-line catholics did; that is from what I observed. I did have an escape, though: singing. I loved to sing. I knew the words to about any song that came on the radio. We listened to albums of all sorts and all genres. Of course, we all had our favorites. Music was a *big* part of our lives. All of the members of the family could sing, except for Pop. He would joke that he could not carry a tune, even if you put it in a bucket. Mom sang when she was young, and she even had a chance to be the girl singer for a Big Band, but chose to marry Pop instead.

My imagination was all I had back then; there were no cell phones, video games, or computers, like there are today. I was the superhero in comics. I also thought that if I ate lots of peanut butter sandwiches, I would grow big enough to play football in the NFL for the Washington Redskins, as they were called at the time. Then I saw a new TV show called "The Love Boat," and that was when I said to my parents that I was going to work on a cruise ship. Pop quickly said that I was going to be the family athlete and go to college. **Pow!** There went that balloon.

CHAPTER 2

I guess eating all those peanut butter sandwiches really did make me gain weight, because I was a very heavy young man. When my mother went to buy my catholic school uniforms, it was the first time that I was referred to as "husky." It really did not become a problem until I started public school when we moved to Chesterfield County, which bordered the city of Richmond, on the south. The first house I could remember was a three-bed-room, one-bathroom house, where we three boys shared a room, using bunkbeds. Two sisters slept in a bedroom upstairs, and my newborn sister was in the master bed-room, with my parents.

I must step to the side, for a moment, and tell you two stories that happened to me while living in that house.

The first happened when our neighbor's police dog, a German Shepherd, was running loose in their yard and I was at our mutual fence. I started to run away from the fence when the dog started barking at me. The dog ran and jumped the fence. I was not paying attention to where I was running. When I stopped looking at the dog and turned around, I ran directly into a thick, metal birdbath that split my head open. The gash was straight across my forehead. I woke up on the sofa, with our police officer neighbor taping my head together. "You look like Frankenstein," my brother Mike added.

The second story is one that my brother-in-law Gerald likes to tell, but this is my book, so here we go. Gerald and Sharon were sitting on a porch swing in our backyard, and I was throwing one of the cobblestones, which surrounded a flower bed, up in the air and yelling, "Wheee!" and letting it hit the ground. Gerald looked over at me and said, "You are going to throw it up and it is going to drop on your head." Of course, I said, "It will not." I threw the cobblestone in the air, and before I could get my breath, that cobblestone hit me right on top of my head. That is where all my problems started. At least, that is what people say. Now that I am embarrassed, back to the story.

When we moved to our new house, it had three bedrooms, two full bathrooms, and an unfinished basement. We eventually finished the basement and added an extra bedroom down there. My middle sister, Sharon, got married, over that summer, to her childhood sweetheart, Gerald. He lived behind us. It was a family joke that he wore a bend in our back fence because he spent so much time leaning on it and talking to her. Even though we had moved farther away, I still attended catholic school. We were close enough to still attend our home church that was across the street from my school, but closer to Pop's job and out of the city, which had started to decline and had become a big worry for the family. I got involved in sports year-round, and the only sport that I seemed to excel in was baseball. I was a catcher and could hit the ball very well. The only thing that was not a given was female recognition. I mean, cut me some slack; puberty was starting to rear its twisted head, and I was far from ready. Do not get me wrong; I was friends with many of the girls my age, but I was not eye-appealing, like the neighborhood sports stars.

I finally got a little attention from a girl named Michelle. We were in the fifth grade together. She was a cheerleader, and we had danced at sports get-togethers, put on by the athletic association. It was our fifth-grade spring concert, and I auditioned for a solo. I was picked to sing the song "Where is Love" from the musical *Oliver*. We had practice for that night's assembly, and I knocked the song out of the park. Michelle came up to me before we left and said that she wanted to be my girlfriend. I was on cloud nine. I was floating the whole way home. It was only two blocks, but my feet never touched the ground. That night, I was all smiles, and I do not think that I could have pushed my chest out any farther without falling forward. Unfortunately, our whirlwind courtship was noticeably short-lived. Michelle broke up with me the next day, after people made fun of her for wanting the "fat kid" to be her boyfriend. I was crushed, to say the least. That would be the first of many heartbreaks I would have to endure because of my looks. I was not a hideous-looking troll, by any means. I had the dark hair, the olive skin, the Italian personality, but I was tipping the scales. Thanks a lot, peanut butter sandwiches!

Chapter 3

I now was starting sixth grade. It was 1980. Around here, sixth through eighth grade is called middle school. Things picked up where they had left off in elementary school, except for the size and population of the place. There were still kids from the neighborhood, but we had the chance to pick electives for the paths we wanted to follow in life. I am sure you are thinking, "Oh, he chose choir." Nope. I took band. The family of my oldest sister's boyfriend (now her husband) all played instruments, and he lent me a trumpet. In the eyes of the school's macho majority, band was more acceptable for guys than choir. However, my transition into middle school was very tough for me. I was not an exceptionally good student and had to repeat the sixth grade, which meant I was now behind all my friends from the neighborhood. I still participated in sports; however, I could not play middle school football until I was in seventh grade. That was a hard pill to swallow, but a county school rule. There was a lot of competition for players between the local county sports associations and the middle schools.

Have you ever been told by your parents not to get in a car with a stranger? Mine did, but what about someone you knew from the neighborhood? I definitely made a <u>big</u> mistake, one foggy morning, while waiting for my late school bus. A young man from the neighborhood, who had repeated a few grades, pulled up to the bus stop in a Chevy Vega and asked if any of us wanted a ride to school. One of my good friends said, "Yes," and I did not want to be left out, so I jumped in the back while those two were in the front. No one was wearing a seatbelt; they were not mandatory back then, but I wish they had been. On the way to school, it was foggy, and the pavement was wet. We had to go down a street that wound through the woods and had an unbelievably bad "S" curve in the middle. We were going too fast when entering the curve. The driver lost control on the dew-covered pavement, and we struck a tree head-on. That tree was later measured to be almost three feet in diameter. When I came to, I found out the driver had received a broken arm and leg from the engine being pushed back and stitches in his face from hitting the windshield. The kid in the passenger seat received a broken femur and facial stitches, the same way. In the back seat, I only remember being thrown sideways in the seat and hitting my head on the hard, molded arm rest. I was woken up by a fire-fighter, but I could not hear him asking me if I was okay. I was stuck in the car; one of my feet had been trapped under the front seat when I was thrown to the floorboard upon hitting the tree. When I was freed from the car, I remember a female police officer taking me toward the ambulance, but she had to let me go and chase one of my friends who was trying to crawl *out* of the ambulance. He was in shock. When she let go of me, I landed flat on my face. I did not notice that one of my feet was pointing in the wrong direction. My leg had been popped out at the hip socket. When they had secured me to a gurney and placed me in the ambulance next to one of my friends, the next thing I saw was a television camera being put in my face. I quickly pulled the sheet up over my head, thinking that my parents would not find out. *(Really?)* The police officers pushed them out of the way and slammed the ambulance door. We were off to the hospital, where they popped my hip back in and I waited for my parents to show up. I luckily only had a concussion and had to wear a leg brace and a neck brace. Mom kept Pop from doing any more physical damage; however, my ears burned for an awfully long time. I still cringe when I hear, "I told you so."

Chapter 4

Now I was in seventh grade, and I made our middle school football team. Pop was thrilled. The only time my mother had a problem with it was when I made my next trip to the ER. While sacking a quarterback, it felt like both of his knees broke my ribs. I remember being laid on the bench while our trainer waited for my pop to get the car. It was so embarrassing because he drove a dark-blue Ford Granada station wagon. They let him drive it onto the track, to where I was lying on the bench. The tailgate lifted upward, and they slid me in the back, headfirst. One of my friends told me that it looked like I was being put in a hearse. The only good thing about the experience was that one of our cheerleaders stayed next to me until "the hearse" showed up.

That year, both of my parents were not happy with the fact that our team was invited to a local college game and the coach let each of us take an "escort." In our family, the kids were not allowed to date until we turned sixteen years old. So, I could not call this a first date. We were a boy and a girl who were friends, attending a football game with a group of other boys and girls, which was the truth.

Somehow, I ended up getting in trouble. The coach told us to meet at the buses as soon as the game was over. My escort and I got there early, and we were accused of sneaking back to the bus to "make out." That was not the case, as God is my witness. I was already on thin ice with my parents about the whole "escort" thing. The coach reported us to the principal and to our parents. The latter was the one that worried me the most. We had already played our last game, so I did not miss anything there, but we both got in-school detention, and I got a lot worse at home. The girl never forgave me for her getting in trouble and word traveled fast at school.

The only thing that saved my middle school years was that two teachers wanted to put on a musical during my eighth-grade school year. I was a big eighth-grader and was already growing a mustache, due to having to repeat the sixth grade. There were not enough boys who could sing at the school or who were even interested. I asked my mom if I could audition, and, of course, she said, "Yes." Before my pop ever found out, I had landed the lead role. It was called *Shenandoah*, a Civil War-era show, and I portrayed "Charlie Anderson," a widower who had a handful of kids. I did the family proud. Mom and Pop were at every show. Pop was even more proud because I was allowed to use a real Civil War rifle, which belonged to James W. Craig. He is my great-great grandfather, and he fought in the Battle of Cold Harbor, in Mechanicsville, Virginia (for the Confederacy, of course).

After that, the Drama teacher at the neighboring high school came and asked if any of us would be interested in trying out for their spring musical. They were doing *Oliver* and needed people to play the orphans. I received permission from my parents, and away I went. I ended up auditioning for a lead role, because I was too big to play an orphan. I beat out a bunch of high school males for the part I was given. Most were juniors and seniors, and they did not like it too much. But hey, I just did my thing. I won the part of "Fagan," a man of seventy years or so, who oversaw a gang of young pick-pockets. Rehearsals started one week after *Shenandoah* ended. What an experience. I was hooked, and at once, I knew that singing and performing was my calling.

CHAPTER 5

I just squeaked by with my grades and was now on my way to high school. I had no idea how much my life would change in the years to come. But ready or not, it was about to hit me full-force. An unexpected opportunity had come my way and would make my high school years a whole lot more enjoyable. My middle brother, Michael, and self-professed "ladies' man" of the family, was dating, and is now married to, a girl named Laura. Yes, we have two Lauras in our family. She used to call me *butterball.* Anyway, she was a rising senior at Meadowbrook High School, the same school that four of the six of us Craig kids attended. She was already a member of the vocal ensemble choir there. It only consisted of juniors and seniors. Unbeknownst to me, Laura had already talked to the chorus teacher at the high school about me and got me an audition. She took me to the high school one day, and, after the audition, the teacher approved me, a rising ninth-grader—the first ninth-grader to ever become a member of the vocal ensemble.

So, when I told my parents about getting into the upper-class student choir, I also had to break the news to Pop that I was going to stop participating in sports. I was just burned-out and not into it anymore, but he convinced me to at least give high school football a try. So, I begrudgingly went and tried out; however, it was as a kicker. I was tired of getting my butt clobbered, play after play, on the line of scrimmage. The first day of practice, the coach came over to me and said that, for the first game, we were playing a team that had a running back about the same size as me. I was like: *okay ... and ... ?* So, I was the tackling dummy for a whole week, plus doing my kicking workout. I never made it to the first game. I turned my equipment in and never looked back. I dealt with the ridicule from the team and joined the marching band.

I do not think my pop ever got over it. I was his last son and his last shot at having an athlete in the family. I was now interacting with close-to-adult females, and I was going through puberty. In our family, we never had "The Talk." That, at least for me, was left up to taking Sex Education during Health and PE class. So, I was learning as I went, but I always heard my pop in my ear, saying, "Do not bring home something that you cannot take care of." That scared the heck out of me. So, I made a deal with myself that I would not engage in intercourse until I was married. Would I make it? We will see.

I can honestly say that my high school years, although they were tough, made me feel that I was making progress toward my future by being in the marching band for two years and singing in the choir all four years. Yet, my grades were still taking a nosedive. Pop said that it was because I could not stop thinking about the girls, and Mom said that I was not applying myself enough. The answer to both was "Yes!"

However, something happened to me when I was around fifteen or sixteen years old that would change a tremendous part of who I was at the time. Remember how I explained that I grew up catholic? Well, the Church was planning to build another church in Chesterfield County, right near where we lived. We were going to be one of the startup families that would be attending that church. They had broken ground, but instead of driving to our usual church, they started having services at the elementary school that my younger sister and I attended. It was two blocks from our house. When the real church was complete, my parents made me start going to Youth Group. It was once a week. I did not learn much, but there was a lot of hooking-up—especially when we went to Pocahontas State Park for a weekend retreat. It was more like a "treat" to everyone. So, even more, my church life was non-existent, at best.

The church that was built was more modern than the old one. One thing it did not have was a confessional. In the old church, we would sit in something the size of a phone booth, and there was a little sliding window with mesh covering it. The priest would sit in an adjoining "phone booth" and slide the little window open when he was ready for us to spill our guts. At the new church, we would go into the vestment room, where the priest and altar servers would get ready for mass. We just sat face-to-face with the priest. I was also an alter server, so I knew the layout well. On one occasion, I had to go to confession, and the associate priest, whom I will not name, was doing confessions that time. I really did not care for him, because he was very touchy-feely. He would come up behind us and rub our shoulders all the time. However, this time in confession, he tried to take it further. We were sitting, facing each other, almost touching knees, and he reached over and placed his hands on my knees while I was talking. I tried to scoot back, but the chair would not move on the carpet. He then started to move his hands up my thighs. That was it! That was when my unquestioned loyalty and beliefs were taken from me. In a face-to-face confession with our associate priest!

I was fifteen or sixteen years old, overweight, and very socially unaccepted (unless I was being funny or singing). The perfect mark for what we know, today, as a predator. The church was something that my parents made me attend, and the farther I sat toward the back, the better. When we grow up catholic, it is instilled in us that there is a "pecking order." It was GOD – the priest – our parents – then us. We were never to question the order, and we were never to question the information that came *down* in that order. But when it felt wrong to me on that particular day, I would not have cared even if that guy were the president. I told him to take his hands off me, or I was going to kill him. Then and there, church was over for me. I played along for my parents' sake until I turned eighteen.

I never told anyone, until sometime in 1993. I mean, who was going to believe me? Certainly not the Church. It would have shamed my parents and family. That is when I took

God's wonderful gift, my voice, did everything I could to become "eye-appealing," and started my trip to what I envisioned was "the good life." I was fortunate enough to make All-County and All-Region Choir for four years, and All-State for my junior and senior years. I made loads of great friends during every event. There are friendships that were made that I still cherish and engage in, to this day.

CHAPTER 6

When I turned sixteen, I was able to have my first real job. Three of my siblings had all held jobs at the area amusement parks. Cindy was a dresser and seamstress for the Broadway-style show, Charlie worked at the front gate, and Mike dressed up as one of the park's characters. We would go to the parks for free, all the time. I was hired as a character. It was a lot of fun, especially when my friends would show up and they could not tell which one I was, until I embarrassed the mess out of them. I was not getting the hours I was hoping for, so I talked to a friend that worked in the games department, and he got me a job in games. I learned a lot about how to win at certain games and which ones were a waste of time. We would go to the competing amusement park and clean them out of prizes. It was also a plus when I took a date to an amusement park or the fair.

I needed to have transportation to get to work though, which was forty-five minutes away from our house. So, I made a deal with Pop, who talked to a car dealer friend of his and got me my first car. It was a used, black Ford EXP with a sunroof. They only made them for two years. This was Ford's attempt to make a two-seater sports car. The only problem I faced with the car was that it had a stick shift, and I had no idea how to drive one. Pop said that this was a life lesson. If I could learn to drive a vehicle with a stick, I would be able to drive anything. Of course, he was right. He parked it in the driveway and made me put it in first and take off, then in reverse and back it up. Back and forth, all day, every day, until my first day of work. Then, I was on my own. Stopping on hills was the worst, but I got the hang of it. I drove that little car until I blew up the engine. I did not know that I had to keep it full of oil. Pop sold it for parts to a man who had another one. He took the money and paid off the car, but I did not get another for a while.

CHAPTER 7

O ne other highlight of my early high school years was
something called Virginia Music Camp. My parents
allowed me to go to a week-long summer camp that was just
for singers. The campers came from all over the state. I not
only came away with invaluable music experience, but I also
made life-long friends and began my "brush" with sexual
attraction from the females. It is where I became part of a
group that, during the first year, was called "The Ju Cru," and
the second year was "The Cru 2," which, I guess by proxy, I
was the leader of. We were not allowed to go during our senior
year, but the members who could go continued the legacy. I
met my female BFF, Kelly, the first summer, and my male BFF,
Tommy, the second summer.

Here is a funny story about how Tommy and I met. I love
telling this story. We still talk and laugh about it, to this day.
At that time, I was really starting to be full of myself. I had
packed my home stereo in the car to put in my room at camp.
I thought I would be rooming with someone I knew. I had
gotten to camp early, set up my stereo, picked my bed. A little
while later, more people started coming by and "checking

in," while I "kicked back" on my bed and blasted my music. Suddenly, this kid walks in, looking lost, with that "deer in the headlights look," and said, "Hi! I'm Tommy, and I'm your roommate." To which I replied, "No, you are not!" I then got up and tried to find out what was going on, but on the way out, I made sure that I told him not to touch my stuff, especially the stereo. I came back to my room, after talking to the head of housing, defeated. This guy named Tommy, with his perfect hair, and looking like he just walked off the pages of Teen Beat Magazine, was now my roommate. It definitely turned out to be the <u>best</u> summer. He was automatically part of the group and my new brother. Tommy even took on the mantle, the following summer at camp, as leader of the group. He even got to go with my family on our beach vacation to Nags Head, North Carolina, where we had started going when Buckroe started to get a little shady. I really did not know how much I would need that experience before my senior year.

CHAPTER 8

The beginning of my senior year did not start off very well. Over the summer, I had noticed a small lump on my right wrist, and my hand began to tingle. My mother took me to the doctor, and we were told that I had what is called a ganglion cyst, which occurs on one's wrist. Since it was making my wrist and hand tingle, it had to be removed. Luckily, I did not have to stay in the hospital. It was an out-patient procedure. I had only a few stitches, and my arm, from the hand to the elbow, was wrapped and braced. It did not stop me from entering a big contest that year. There used to be a show on television called *Puttin' on the Hits*. People would go on the show and impersonate their favorite performing artists. They had to look, as much as possible, like those artists and then lip-sync to one of their songs. Well, they were coming to our state fair and, of course, I wanted to compete. With the support of my parents and a chorus friend named Ellen, I dressed up as the late Kenny Rogers. Mom made me a fake beard to go with my mustache that I had been growing since the sixth grade, and sprayed my hair with silver hair spray, and away we went. I performed the song "Lady." There was a big stage on the front stretch of the racetrack, and the stands were packed with people. It was my first taste of performing in front of a huge crowd. I absorbed it like a sponge. I did not want it to end. I came in the top three, but unfortunately, I did not win. However, the experience was invaluable and made me want to perform for a living all the more.

I kept struggling with my grades and had to attend summer school a few times to stay with the same class. My terrible grades even caused me to miss the lead role in the school musical, my junior year. They did *The Sound of Music*, and I was being looked at to play the role of "Captain Von Trapp." The principal said that if my grades were not up to passing, I had no chance. All the same, my senior year was going to be a different story. I had already made it very well-known to my parents that college was not in my future, and not just because of my low grades, but by choice. I was out to prove to everyone that I was going to be someone in the entertainment field.

I had been the Master of Ceremonies at the high school beauty pageant, as well as a few others done in the local area. I had even gotten a girlfriend, who was a state queen, named Tammy.

The musical my senior year was going to be *South Pacific*, and I knew it well. There are four lead roles, and one was going to be mine. I succeeded and landed the role of Lieutenant Cable. I would have to take my shirt off while on stage. I had never taken my shirt off in front of anyone, except my family and in the locker-room. Halfway through that year, I had started losing weight, which was fine with me. I did not know why, but I was not complaining.

In *South Pacific*, I had to kiss my love interest many times and have a heavily edited love scene. Her name was Katie, and we went to the same church, sang together in the school choir, and were in the marching band. We were friends, but we had the same problem. We were each dating someone, and they were not too happy about us kissing. We had a challenging time doing the kissing scenes in front of the cast, so our director and school Drama teacher, whose name was Priscilla, took us both into her room for a talk. When we got in there, she said that we had to get over it and just get it done, then she grabbed me and laid one on me. Not Katie, but Priscilla, the teacher. After overcoming the initial shock, and Katie stopped laughing, Priscilla said, "Look; it's over, and I'm not in love with him. Now, get over yourselves; it is called "acting" for a reason." After that, we did not worry about it and enjoyed it. Just to spite being in trouble with the people we were dating, we added a few more smooches to the shows. Priscilla was right; all of us got over it.

Chapter 9

My good friend and castmate at the time, Paul, was dating Tammy's best friend, Deanna, so we double-dated. I took Tammy to my Senior Prom and made the most uneducated decision that I had ever made, up to that moment, in my life. I thought that she was "the one" and gave her a ring. Paul and Deanna knew and tried to talk me out of it. Tammy accepted. Boy, was I ever sorry.

After not graduating, I had to have my second surgery. I had lost so much weight, so quick, and was having a pain in my lower back. Mom took me to the doctor, and he found that I had a pilonidal cyst, which was located just at the start of my buttocks, right on the base of my spine. It was the size of a pea, but when they finally did the surgery, they found out that it was the shape of a triangle and was growing between my vertebrae, hence the back pain.

A week after the surgery, my back started to hurt me badly, in the same spot. Back to the doctor we went, and my incision had abscessed. So, the doctor had me lie on my stomach right there in his office exam room and cut my incision back open. The next thing I knew was I was being wheeled out of the office front door, across the street, and toward the hospital. It is good that my doctor's office was on the same campus as the hospital.

Even though I was eighteen by then, I requested to be put in the pediatric wing. They had taken such loving care of me before, that I felt safer there. The head nurse was named Debbie, who I am still friends with today. She used to sneak Snickers bars up to me every time she worked.

I would say that I was in the hospital for about a week. They had to leave my incision open so it could heal from the inside out. They would pack it with gauze soaked in betadine and change it every four to six hours. They had to teach my mom how to do it because when I left the hospital, she would become my nurse.

A few of my friends would come to see me, besides Tammy. Eddie, a close friend at the time, came by. I knew that he went to the same hangouts that Tammy and I would go to, so I asked him if he would keep an eye on Tammy for me. Boy, did he keep an eye on her. Tammy and I had argued about her going to "Beach Week" after graduation. One night when she had come to the hospital, she was wearing a dress that she had bought to take with her. Skintight and left nothing to the imagination. Remember, she was a beauty queen. She told me that I had no say and that she was going and wearing the dress.

After being released from the hospital, I was home-bound for about two weeks. Mom did an excellent job with taking care of my wound.

One day, my BFF Tommy surprised me and came to the house. He convinced my parents that I needed to get out of there, so he took me back to spend the night at his house. My mom made him watch her change my dressing. He still never lets me live that down. Imagine having to lie across a bed and have your mom pack gauze in a hole just above your butt, with your best friend watching.

When I came back from Tommy's, I had a call from Eddie. He told me that he and Tammy had "hooked-up" and were now dating. Right then, I got up and got in the car and drove over to Tammy's. I asked if it was true, and she said, "Yes," very calmly and coldly. She told me that Eddie had told her what I had said to him, and he was at "Beach Week," where they got together. So, I demanded the ring back and everything else that she had of mine and got back in the car. Just as I was getting ready to leave, Eddie pulled up and was stepping out of his car. I got back out and started to run toward him. Tammy jumped in between us, and her father had come out, and he grabbed me. Of course, I was blessing Eddie out and trying to get my hands on him, but he had jumped back in his car, and Tammy's father was ushering me to mine. I think I would have ripped Eddie's head off.

I look back on it, now, and think about how foolish I looked, but also, I remember Eddie. He was a good friend and quite a character. A few years later, he drove his car off a bridge near where I lived and was killed. R.I.P., Eddie.

CHAPTER 10

I had finally proved to my pop that I needed another car. So, again, he went to a dealership where he bought his cars, and his friend told him that we were in luck. A car had just been traded in and we could get it at a decent price. This time, Pop made me make the car payments, and he would pay the insurance. It was a dream car. A 1984 white Ford Mustang convertible, with white leather interior, white top, and blue carpet. It was also an automatic. Pop was not too sure about it, but I was. I loved that car and kept it washed, waxed, and running well. I had learned my lesson from last time.

Right down the road from our house, there was a dinner theatre called The Swift Creek Mill Playhouse, and they were holding auditions for an upcoming musical. I went down there and won a part in their next production, *Fiddler on the Roof*. I would wait tables before the show, then go upstairs and perform. The money was okay, but I knew that I had to pay my dues if I wanted to do this for a living. I was enjoying performing in the show, but one day, they put a flyer on the backstage door about upcoming auditions for a cruise ship in the Caribbean. I thought, *what the heck, it would be wonderful experience and look good on a resume.*

I went into the audition, wanting to do my best and receive some constructive criticism. I dressed nice and was prepared, or so I thought. I did not know that I had to have sheet music for two songs, one fast and one slow. It was the beginning of the karaoke era, so I had pre-recorded tracks for my songs. After being told that was not how auditions worked, they still let me audition. There were three people on the panel. One male and two females. I recognized one of the females as Liz. She had her own one-woman show and performed around town. The other two were partners and built shows for cruise ships. Their company was called G&C Entertainment. They were out of New York City. I got through the fast song, then one of the people from New York, Greg, spoke up and said that I had to sing the song to Liz, and make her get goose bumps. I said, "Okay," and as soon as the song started, I locked eyes with Liz. It was not hard, because she was extremely attractive. After I was finished, she smiled, rolled her eyes, and fanned herself. My cockiness was short-lived when Connie got up and asked me if I had any dance experience. I said, "No, ma'am." Then she said, "Well, let us see you move." She showed me a few steps and I repeated them. Then she made me perform spins from one corner of the room to the other without stopping. I really felt like a fool.

The audition was over, and they said that they were holding auditions at Virginia Commonwealth University here in Richmond, and also in New York City. I thought, "Great.

I'm glad I was not getting my hopes up." They then explained that if I were going to be offered the job, I would hear something in the next week. I thanked them and left to get ready for that night's performance.

Exactly one week later, I received a call from New York. It was Greg, and my heart skipped a beat. He explained that for the job I auditioned for, G&C had around eighty other males vying for that one position. I was ready for the next words to be, "Sorry, kid."

Mom was standing next to me and straining to hear what was being said while she cooked dinner. The next thing I knew, I was asking Greg to repeat what he had said. He repeated that they were offering me the cruise ship job. My "Love Boat" prediction had come true! I yelled into the phone, that yes, I would except the offer! Greg said they knew I was green, but they were willing to take a chance on me. He then went on to explain that I would be receiving my contract to sign and would be gone until September. I would also need a passport. I did not have one, and with only two weeks to get a passport, my parents had to drive me up to Washington, D.C. We went straight to the passport office with my contract the next day. They expedited the paperwork, and I had my passport.

My pay was going to be awesome, in my mind at least. Pop told me to see what else I needed when I got there and to start sending money home to keep up with the car payments. Three hundred dollars per week, in cash, and it would be tax-free. All my room and board were included. Along with my contract were the lyrics on paper and a tape of my parts of the show. They would be flying me to meet the ship in Montego Bay, Jamaica, in two weeks. *(Two weeks?)* That is all the time I had to learn all my songs, plus I had to have two solo pieces, which would be incorporated into the shows.

Within a couple of days, a package the size of a shirt box arrived. Everything I was expecting was there; also, a list of clothes I would need, as well as other necessities, were in there. The clothes were no problem because, thankfully, I was working at Chess King. It was a hip clothing store in the 1980s. I did some in-store modeling for them and got to keep the clothes. My wardrobe had to consist of: three suits with shirts and ties, a full black tuxedo, a few pairs of white pants, white lace-up shoes, and black dress shoes that would double as my performing shoes. Then I could bring whatever else I wanted for regular clothes.

I then went to the local music store and found the sheet music for my solos. I chose "She's Like the Wind" by Patrick Swayze and I already had "Truly" by Lionel Richie. I, thankfully, had a cassette tape player in my car, so, everywhere I went, I was rehearsing.

Chapter 11

I had the hard job of telling the playhouse that I was leaving. The show was only halfway through the run, and the director did not take it very well. When I returned after my tour, they had black-balled me from ever coming back. Oh, well; I was off to do bigger and better things. Mom was bragging to everyone, but I could see that Pop still was not too sure about making a living this way.

At the time, I was dating Jenny, a girl from a neighboring county. I had met her at a band competition. I hung out at her house as much as I could. Her mother, Jan, would get me to sing all the time because Jan played the piano. Jan was a very devout Christian, and she had me sing at some of her church's functions. She would talk to me about faith. I listened, but still did not understand that much. I really enjoyed those talks, though. When I told them I had been given a job on a cruise ship, Jan was ecstatic. Jenny was not upset, because she did not see me as a boyfriend; she was happy that I was following my dream.

Before I left, Mom had a little going-away party for me at our house. It was just our family, Jan and her kids, and a few of my parents' friends. I was flying out the next morning, and after packing everything that I owned in the world, I asked my parents if I could go over to Jan and Jenny's and hang out with them. Jenny's brothers, C.W. and Michah, were already in bed. Jan said that she had something for me to take on my trip. She came back with a Bible, which had my name embossed on the cover, and a modern-looking, silver crucifix. Jan asked me to wear it to keep me safe. It was really cool, and I never took it off. I stayed at their house all night, and when it was time to leave, Jan said she wanted to go to the airport to see me off. Jenny got a little teary-eyed when I left, but said she already had plans with her friends that morning and would not be coming to the airport. That was the last time I saw Jenny. Jan and I, however, are still friends today.

It was April 23, 1988; my flight was at six o'clock that morning, out of Richmond International Airport. I was excited, but very anxious. This was the first time I would be away from my family for more than a week. Mom, Pop, and Jan were there to see me off. After a few tears, I boarded the plane for the unknown. I first had to fly to Atlanta, Georgia and change planes to fly to Jamaica. On the plane, I met a gentleman by the name of Gary. He was going to the same place I was and said that he would help me out. What a relief! He was going to be the saxophone player on the same ship as I was going to be on. He helped calm my nerves about my luggage, also. I had five bags and had never been responsible for all of this by myself before.

When we landed in Atlanta, our flight was late, so we had to run halfway across the airport for our connecting flight. If you have never been to the Atlanta airport, let me tell you: it is <u>massive.</u> We made it just in time and actually had seats near one another. So, Gary tried to let me in on what to expect, because he had done this before. Our second flight was very rowdy. It was filled with lots of vacationers who had already started to get their party on. I had just turned twenty years old on March thirty-first. So, it was a Coke and peanuts for me.

I almost pulled my armrests off of my seat when we made our approach to the Montego Bay airport. The plane had to come in extremely low, and we were over the water. The water in the Caribbean is eight shades of blue and so clear. We were so close to it that I thought I saw fish. Finally on the ground and at the gate, it was time to exit. I was wearing a lightweight jacket over a short-sleeved shirt because it was still cool back home and on the plane. Gary got up first, and I followed close behind him. When I made it to the door of the plane, the heat hit me like a ton of bricks. One-thousand percent humidity. I was sweating before I got to the steps.

Gary helped me find all of my bags, and we hopped in a shuttle van that was waiting for us. It was one of those small Toyota passenger vans, and our driver looked like he had just stepped off of a reggae album. After everyone was in the van, the driver jumped in, and we were off like a bullet out of a gun. He was swerving and dodging through the streets, narrowly avoiding people and animals.

When we made it to our destination in what seemed like five seconds, we were facing our ship. It was surrounded by a tall fence and heavily-armed soldiers. I looked at Gary, and he said for me not to worry and told me that the soldiers were there to keep people from trying to stow away on the ships. I had started to calm down a little bit, which was until he explained to be ready for them to search my bags. I had five bags; I hoped they would wave me through, or the ship would leave without me! Luckily, all they did was give me "The Stare," and off I went.

I followed Gary up to an open door on the side of the ship, where I gave my passport to one of the ship's officers and he checked me off his list. He was from Greece. I would find out that all of the officers were Greek, all the way up to the captain. This officer took a keen interest in the cassette tape carrier that I had brought along. He stopped me and asked if he could look inside. He was speaking to me in broken English and asked if he could listen to what I had in there sometime. I told him that he could anytime. He must have thanked me a dozen times as I walked away and into what I would call "home" for the summer.

CHAPTER 12

The ship was called the S.S. Britanis, one of the ships in the Chandris Fantasy Cruise Ship Fleet. All the ships were painted the same way. They were a bright white with blue trim and had an "X" on each smokestack with their names on their bows, in blue. S.S. Britanis's registry was in the Bahamas, where the fleet was based. She was five stories tall, sat thirty-eight feet deep in the water and was three hundred feet wide at her widest. Her length was as long as two and a half football fields. During World War II, she was commissioned as a troop carrier.

The "Brit," as I would grow to call her, could carry up to fifteen hundred passengers and had a crew of five hundred. The crew was a tremendous mix of nationalities, languages, and skin colors. It was going to be a marvelous opportunity for me. I could not wait to get started. There was a lot to learn and a brief time to learn it. The first night on board, I met the other performers who I would work with in the show, along with the out-going cast. There was a five-piece backup band, six female dancers from England and Scotland, a magician named Bob, a female singer from New York named Deb, a male singer named Ray (also from New York), and Chris, the sound engineer.

We had dinner together with Connie and Greg that night. I was sitting next to Ray and made a very startling discovery within the first five minutes of dinner. I really stuck my foot in my mouth and wanted to crawl under the table afterwards. I had noticed, while doing the show at the dinner theatre, most of the performers were gay. I was innocent to this, but knew that in the theatre it was quite common. So, I leaned over to Ray and said, "Ray, may I ask you something?" He responded, "Sure, anything." Here is where I opened my mouth and inserted my foot. I said, "Ray, What do you think about all these gay people?" Ray turned to me and said, in a matter-of-fact way, "I love them." I did not know what to say next, so I decided to be quiet for the rest of the meal. I did not find out until later who Ray was. You see, Ray turned out to be none other than Ray Stephens from the Village People. He played the part of the police officer and sang lead. He was also part of a children's show called *The Great Space Coaster*.

We did not have our room assignments yet, so our luggage was stored in a passenger room near the ballroom. However, by the end of dinner, I was told that Ray and I would be roommates. The new cast would stay in passenger cabins until we would move to our staff lodgings on the very top of the ship after the current cast left.

There was no rehearsal that night, so I roamed around the ship and tried to make sure that this was not a dream. The ship was late leaving port, and it was dark outside on deck, but there were people everywhere.

As I walked up the stairs from the dining room, I entered what was called the lounge area, or disco. That is where I would end up spending most of my free time. There was a DJ playing all types of music, and the bar was crowded. I even recognized some of the people from our flight.

As I walked out of the back door, I saw the pool and sunbathing area. The pool was surprisingly small, and there were balloons sitting on top of the water. Staff was not allowed in the pool at any time, or in the sunbathing area, I found out later. The entertainment staff had their own sunbathing area. It was called "Metal Beach." It was on top of the ship, directly above our cabins.

Within a few minutes of walking around on deck, I was approached by a young female, about my age, who was with her mother. They were taking a cruise together, just the two of them, and they asked me why I was walking around alone. I explained that I worked on the ship and that I would be performing in the shows starting the following week. They said that it sounded exciting and wished me well. After talking for about thirty minutes, I started to walk away. As I was walking away, the mother came up to me and said that if I wanted to, I could meet them back at their cabin later, because they "shared everything," and gave me a wink. She told me the room number, but I was still trying to get over the first part.

I kept walking around and ended up on the sun deck. It was an open-air deck with a railing that wrapped around the top. It was located above the wheelhouse. That is where the captain would steer the ship. It ran from one side of the ship to the other. I saw the "mother-daughter duo" up there and made sure that I was out of sight.

On the dock area was a Jamaican marching band. They were playing, dancing, and waving up at the ship. At that very second, the ship's horn blew, and I went deaf for a minute. It meant that the ship was getting ready to leave the dock. I was starting my adventure. I hoped it would be all that I expected it to be.

CHAPTER 13

It was around midnight when the ship finally left port. I wandered around for about an hour or so more. I then ran into Ray, Deb, and others from the show, in the lounge. Ray bought me a drink. He said, "Young man, you better get used to it. It will be your best friend," referring to the drink. I had sipped alcohol at my parents' parties, and I also had Slow Gin with my brothers while we went sledding down Government Hill, back home. However, this was something entirely different. It was sweet but packed a wallop; by the time I finished it, my head was spinning, and I did not know if it was the ship rocking or just me. It was time for me to go, after finishing my drink. So, I said thanks to Ray and goodnight to everyone else and headed for my room. As I was leaving, I remember Ray yelling to me, "You get the top bunk."

Before I made it back to the room, I saw "The Duo" walking down the hall with some gentleman in tow. I shook my head and chuckled.

I was already in bed when Ray came back. He told me that we had a meeting with Connie and Greg the next morning, then he collapsed on his bed, still dressed.

When I woke up the next morning, I did not know if it was light outside yet. Our room was in the interior of the ship, and it was pitch-black. After getting cleaned up, I headed to breakfast. Some of the cast members were already there with Connie and Greg. They all said, "Good morning," and asked how I slept. Even though my head was pounding, I smiled and said that I slept well. I really did sleep great on the ship; it was very soothing. Connie said that rehearsals would start that very night in the ballroom at one o'clock in the morning. After breakfast, we were allowed to disembark from the ship at our first port.

My first week on the ship was like a working vacation. During the day, we got to do the tourist-type things, and after six in the evening, we would shadow the people we would be replacing.

At one o'clock in the morning, we would rehearse. Just in my first week on the ship, I got to visit Montego Bay, Jamaica; Cartagena, Colombia; San Blas, which is a tiny island about the size of the ship, where we had a beach party; and, finally, a port on Grand Cayman. Did you know that in Grand Cayman is a place called Hell? It is a bunch of rock formations that are sticking out of the ground. The rocks looked like burnt tree stumps of different heights that were sharp on the top and had murky water running through it. There was even a post office, and they sold postcards from Hell. I sent some home saying that I had been to Hell and back. I could not resist.

A funny story, I must tell you, was not so funny at the time, but now as I look back on it, it was. I was so naïve back then. We were in Cartagena Colombia and on our way back to the ship. Ray came up to me and asked me to take a package back to the ship for him. I already had my hands full with bags of fresh coffee and a stuffed-animal parrot to hang in my room. I still took the package from him. The package looked about a foot long and shaped like a loaf of bread. It was sealed up in brown paper. We had to walk past armed guards before getting back on the ship. They stopped me and asked to see the coffee and even smelled the parrot. I was told by two of the people I was with that they were checking for contraband, like cocaine or marijuana. They gave me my stuff back and I walked onto the ship and to my room.

Ray came into the room a few minutes after me, thanked me, and asked for the package. He opened it right there, and that is when I saw and smelled marijuana for the first time in my life. I was Ray's "drug mule!" And I was still a virgin. What the heck? That was the last time I ever carried anything for anyone back to the ship!

CHAPTER 14

After that experience, I decided that I should try to make some close friends who knew their way around and could show me the ropes. The sports director was from Canada, and his name was Sandro. He was Italian, like me, so we hit it off right away. The show's magician was from Jacksonville, Florida, and his name was Bob. Those two were familiar with working on cruise ships, and we became inseparable. "The Three Amigos!" My first week was over, and I already had stories to tell the folks back home, but it was also time to take the reins of the shows.

Connie and Greg would stay one more week to watch and critique what needed to be worked on. The tour that the ship would take from our home port of Miami, Florida, would be Key West, Florida; then Playa Del Carmen, Mexico; Cozumel, Mexico; a day at sea; and then back in Miami. The weekend would be spent in the Bahamas. This is what our schedule looked like. It was both a good thing and a terrible thing. Sunday, we would leave Miami at four thirty in the afternoon; the "Captain's Cocktail Party" was that night. There were two of them to accommodate seating everyone, and we were expected to be at both, with drinks in our hands. They only served two types of alcoholic drinks at the party, Gin Fizz or Martinis. The entertainers were the ambassadors of the ship. We would interact the most with the passengers, out of all the crew. We were in Key West on Monday morning until around twelve thirty in the afternoon; then, we would head toward Mexico.

Monday night was our first set of shows. I do not know why I did this little ritual before every show, but I would stick my head in between the backstage wall and the speaker and say an "Our Father" and a "Hail Mary." I really did not know how to pray, so I pulled these two out from my catholic school days. They were all I had. I wanted to pay respect to whoever got me here.

Tuesdays, we were in what was a small town then, Playa del Carmen. It was on the mainland of Mexico, south of Cancun. In the town where tourists could buy silver, hand-made crafts, and other knick-knacks. When we first got to the dock, we had to maneuver through a throng of kids selling gum. The beach was, of course, breathtaking. White sand and crystal-clear water. The tourists would spend time together on the beach right in front of the town. However, the crew would walk about five hundred yards down the beach. There was a square bar there, called Costa Del Mar. It was located at a topless beach, where we, the crew, could get away from the passengers.

We would drink and snack all day. That night on the ship, we had a costume party. There were no shows that night.

Sometimes the passengers would bring their own costumes, but if they did not, we helped them come up with something. We would line up everyone who was in a costume and parade them across the stage while the people in the audience were screaming for their favorites.

The next day was Wednesday. We were on the island of Cozumel. It was straight off the coast of Playa. There was more to do here for everyone. Bars, clothes, loose gemstones, diamonds, and quite a few good restaurants. There was a place that Sandro, Bob, and I would always go to. It had no front wall. And looked like an old 'fifties soda shop. It was called "Studebaker's." That night was our "French Show." Everything was French-themed; our dancers even did the Can-Can. I had a solo in French. Did I know what I was singing about? Nope.

Thursdays were called a "Day at Sea," because that is exactly what it was: an entire day at sea. We did not see any land at all. That night was our "Finale Show." In it, we said farewell to the passengers before they left the ship on Friday. Some passengers would stay on for the weekend, or new passengers would board the ship Friday afternoon.

When we left on Friday afternoon at four thirty, our destination was Nassau, in the Bahamas. Friday night, we would perform the same shows that we did on Monday nights. On Saturday, we would spend all day, up until six o'clock that evening, in Nassau. Then we would repeat Thursday night's shows on Saturday night. If you were on the ship for seven days, you saw shows repeated.

Now I have to tell you about the dressing room—yes, I said dressing room, singular. Six dancers, three singers, and a magician all dressed in about a ten-foot square room—and that is being generous—at the same time. One hook per person. There was no time or place for modesty. The first rehearsal on the ship was my first time ever seeing a fully nude woman, but during the show, there was no time to look, anyway. The dancers' costumes took up most of the room. Their headpieces were enormous and weighed a ton. Those young ladies had to have extraordinarily strong necks. Jackie, the lead dancer and show boss, put one on my head once. It dang-near broke my neck. And they had to wear them while walking in heels! I grew to think of all of them as my sisters. All of them referred to me as a "Cheeky Monkey."

Chapter 15

After the first month, I was starting to get bored. Every day was the same thing. Every Monday, I could tell you what they would serve for dinner, because it was the same every Monday. Monday's menu was also served on Friday night, and Thursday's menu was served Saturday night. The only thing that changed were the people. If you worked on the ship, you had to become creative, so that you would not get bored.

The first few months, I was sending money home, but then I started drinking to pass the time and gambling in Nassau. On the ship, crew members only had to pay half of their bar tabs. It would be taken out of our pay. To get around this, we would buy liquor in the Bahamas, dirt-cheap, and store it in our closets. It was the same for sodas, and even foods.

In the middle of June, I met a passenger who threw me for a loop. She had come on the ship with her high school graduating class. When I first saw her, she was in the lounge, playing a drinking game with her friends. Sandro, Bob, and I were there, scoping out the week's prospects. Her name was Dawn. She had shoulder-length, blonde, wavy hair and a Florida tan.

She was a little shorter than I was, but looked very athletic. I would later find out that she was a cheerleader. I could not stop looking at her. She saw me looking, and I said that I wanted to talk to her. The place was so loud that I do not even know why I said anything; she could not hear me. She just shook her head yes and kept on playing the drinking game.

That night, I saw her at the "Captain's Cocktail Party." Unfortunately for me, my job was to walk around the ballroom and greet guests, so I lost sight of her. I did not see her again until our first show on Monday night. She and her friends were sitting front-row-center. That night, I said two "Our Fathers" and two "Hail Mary's."

After the first show was over, we went down to the lounge until it was time for the second show. There she was, surrounded by her friends. I got up the nerve and went over and asked her to come to the second show so I would have someone to sing to. She said that she would think about it and gave me a little grin. I told her not to think too long, or the seats would be gone. Then I turned and went back upstairs to the dressing room. When we came out for the first number, there she was, front-row-center. When I came out to sing my solo number, "She's Like the Wind" from the movie *Dirty Dancing*, I made sure that I made eye contact with her every chance I could. When I came out after the show, she was gone. So I went to bed, hopeful about the next day.

I was very tired that night, and as I was climbing into my bunk, I heard girls' voices coming from the stairs outside of our porthole window. At that time, our room was on top of the ship. At one end of our hallway was a door that opened onto the sundeck, right above the wheelhouse. I went outside in shorts and a t-shirt, and there was Dawn and two of her friends. It had started to rain, and they were sitting on the sundeck with their backs against the wall, facing the front of the ship.

I walked over to her and said that it was not a good idea to be sitting out there in the rain. She stood up and grabbed me by the hand. I walked her inside and to my room. Ray had not come back yet, so we were alone. I offered her my beach towel to dry off. I was experiencing a very strange feeling in that moment. I invited her to stay and warm up. She leaned over and kissed me. A kiss like I had never experienced before. Actually, I really did not have much experience at all. It was very passionate and made me feel very warm.

We ended up in my bunk, and that night, I gave up my innocence to a young lady that made the earth move—and it was not because of the ship rocking. Ray would end up walking in on us. Oops.

Dawn spent the rest of her cruise with me. I showed her all the sights and even helped her gamble a little. I was not allowed to gamble on the ship, but I could stand by her and help. When it was time to go, promises were made to write to each other very soon.

It was the Monday night of the next week that I received a message from the wheelhouse. I was requested to come there immediately after finishing that night's shows. I still do not know how I made it through the second show; however, I did, and then literally ran to the wheelhouse. A large Greek officer, whom we called "Gorilla George," was on duty, and he said that I had a ship-to-shore phone call. My heart sank to my feet. What had happened at home? Did someone pass away? Pop's mother and father were the only still-living grandparents I had. *Was there an accident?* I was reeling.

George handed me the phone and said, "Here's your call," in very deep, broken English.

Tentatively, I said, "Hello?"

Now, I must explain that I was not ready for this phone call in the first place, but ship-to-shore calls are very odd. The person on the other end sounds like the adults in the "Charlie Brown" cartoons. You know, "Wah-Wah-Wah." Still, I could understand the words that were being said, and I had to say, "Over," when I had finished speaking.

The voice on the other end said, "Christopher? Over."

And I said, "Yes, who is this? Over."

It was Dawn, calling from her house in Florida. I was both relieved and puzzled. She said, "Can you hear me, ok? Over."

Then I said, "Yes, I can hear you. What is wrong? Over."

She came back, "Nothing, I just wanted to tell you that I love you and that last week was the best time that I had ever had in my life. I asked my mother if I could call you and see if I could come down to the port when you returned on Friday. Over."

After picking my jaw up off the floor, I said, "Sure, and I love you too. Over."

George was looking at me with a stern gaze, and he said that calls were for emergency use only, so I had to wrap it up. I explained that to Dawn, and we agreed on a time to meet. Every Friday and Sunday is when we pulled into port.

Most of the crew would go to an outdoor mall across the port bridge into Miami. We would do laundry, buy necessities, or just get off the ship. We did not need to be back until four o'clock, at the latest. The port of Miami had an Olympic-size swimming pool just for the crew members from the ships. There was also a place to make phone calls and send and receive mail. Dawn and her mother, Ellen, met me at the pool. We had decided to just go swimming because I could do my laundry on Sunday. We had a wonderful time. We talked non-stop about everything, but mostly, our feelings. She told me that in the fall, she would be attending the University of Florida. I told her there was a chance I would be signed on to do the next tour and it would take me away from Miami. She said that she understood but would come down and see me whenever and wherever I happened to end up. We were officially an item.

Chapter 16

N ow, the ship afforded its crew members a luxury that I took full advantage of. We could have guests come on the ship, and they would only pay forty dollars a day. Dawn would take many weekend trips, and we would split the cost, or she would just come down and hang out with me on one of the days that I was in port. Some members of my family took a seven-day cruise, and I asked Dawn to come with them. I wanted them to meet her because our relationship was progressing very rapidly. When I spoke to my mother just before they came down, she said that Dawn could share a room with my younger sister, Laura. I knew, at once, that Mom and I would need to have a serious talk.

Back to Dawn and me. When our meeting was over, there were a lot of tears shed, and she said she would write me, and I said I would call her on Sunday. It was the time of no cell phones. We purchased minutes on calling cards that we used on payphones. I could not tell you how many of those things we burnt up. She did tell me that the first phone call, the ship-to-shore one, had cost her mother three hundred dollars. Ellen would hold that over my head for a long time.

I returned to the ship and resumed my duties, but things had changed my perspective, or so I thought. As I said before, my job was to entertain the guests. They came first. No one cared if you were spoken for. "What happened on the ship stayed on the ship." (Now, I understood the "Dynamic Duo" from my first night.) The veterans in the cast were already used to the program. I, on the other hand, was not. I really let things get out of hand, and I would eventually find myself in trouble with more than a few cast members.

It started on a show night. I had been out drinking with Sandro and Bob, and my stomach had started to cramp very badly. So, I excused myself and said that I was going to bed. I was fast asleep after a long visit to the bathroom, when Ray came into the room. He was in his typical drunken state. I just ignored him and tried to go back to sleep. Ray had other plans.

He came over to our bunkbeds and said, "Hey, Chris, I need to talk to you."

To which I replied," Go to bed, Ray; you are drunk."

He ignored me and then grabbed my leg and said, "Come on, man. I need to talk to you," as he tried to pull me over on my back. I was on my side, facing the wall, with my back to him.

I pulled away and said, "Ray, you are drunk, and I'm not feeling well, so go to sleep or I'm going to deck you!"

He grabbed my leg a little higher and said, "Do not be like that, my friend. Let us just talk."

I warned him. When he pulled on my leg, I turned over and hit him square in the face. I knocked him out, and he landed up under the sink in our cabin. This was the second time that he had made me feel uncomfortable. The first time was when I had come back to our room, and he was in bed with another male crew member. I took the blame, and rightly so, for walking in on them and for striking Ray.

The next day, I was relocated to a room by myself on a passenger deck. Now, you might be thinking that, maybe, this would not be so bad. Sorry, you would be wrong, because it just added to my reckless and self-gratifying behavior. I was a performer on the ship, but we also had crew duties. They were very menial ones, but still part of the job. I had to man the ridiculously small library and check out books for the passengers. Most of the time, no one would come by, except some of the older set. It was a grueling task for me. No excitement. I would either fall asleep or forget to show up altogether. I would then get talked to by my on-ship boss and lead dancer, Jackie. She was petite, with a close-cut bob hair style, but she was a spitfire if we made her mad. I knew this very well, because of my immature actions.

We also had lifeboat drills before leaving our home port every Friday and Sunday. It was mandatory and regulated by the Coast Guard. It was fun because we could joke around with the passengers. I used to act like I was an airplane attendant giving the "pre-flight" instructions. The passengers loved it. But then, I was caught by Jackie. I never did it again. I started taking the "passengers come first" saying way too far. I *was* making sure that the passengers were having a fun time. Especially, the females.

On one cruise, a middle-aged woman was taking a cruise without her husband. She asked me to dance at the cocktail party. She would come to the shows, and I was her company for her time on the ship. When she left, I was called to the front desk and received a package that she had left for me. I opened it, and there was a Gucci watch with a granite face. She had bought it from the ship's duty-free store. There was a note that said, "Thank you for the memorable trip." She only signed it, "Your dance partner."

Bob and Sandro had noticed me burning the candle at both ends. They even pranked me one time by having a woman mail a letter to me when she got home. They had her write that she had a wonderful time in my company, and that she was pregnant with my baby, and that she and her parents were coming to the port next Friday to meet me. I received the letter on a Friday and did not say a word to anyone. Bob and Sandro could barely contain themselves because I was squirming like a worm. My attitude was one of paranoia all week. I hardly came out of my room. I only came out for shows and to eat. That really had my stomach hurting. I went to the ship's doctor and had to get anxiety medicine. I never told Dawn, either. I guess she will know after reading this if she happens to.

I kept a lot of things from her. My drinking was in a bad place. I was only twenty years old, but could drink when the ship was in international waters. I could hang with the best of them. One time, we went to the crew bar in Playa, and they had a drinking contest. The bar was a perfect square, and they had set up double shots called, "Cucarachas." It had tequila, kalua, and cola that was layered in a tall shot glass. We had to cover the glass with a napkin and slam it on the bar to make it fizz, and then "shot it." The bartenders could space out thirty-four of these mindblowers evenly around the bar. The contest was to see who could down the most drinks in one hour without stopping or getting sick. I was going to win, just to prove that I could. I did end up winning. I finished all thirty-four with a little time to spare. As the winner, I was presented a glass goblet that I would drink triples out of for the rest of my tour.

On the other hand, what I had to deal with after the contest was downright scary. I was so drunk that I could not hold my own head up. I still had to walk the five-hundred yards, in the baking sun, back to the dock to catch the tender or water taxi back to the ship and still work the costume party that night. When I made it to the dock, one of the dancers saw me and said she would make sure I got back to my room. When I got to my door, I did not know it was cracked open. I put my hand up on the door, it gave way, and I landed on my face, knocking over a potted plant, which spilled all over the place and me. I was out for the count. There is a picture, out there somewhere, of the porter vacuuming the dirt off of the floor and me.

When I finally came to, it was time for the costume party, and I was still drunk. Bob and Sandro dressed me up in a sombrero and draped a Mexican blanket across me, then they sat me in a chair at the entrance to the ballroom. I did not remember anything after the drinking contest. I only remember waking up the next morning. They almost took me to the infirmary because I was so out of it. The next morning, I will leave to your imagination.

After that, Sandro, Bob, and I would have our own "Cucaracha" parties. We would all chip in and buy the liquor we needed, and we hijacked the glasses from one of the ships' bars. There were so many bars that I am sure that three tall shot glasses were not missed. We would have at least one "Cucaracha" party a week and sometimes one on the weekends.

CHAPTER 17

It was getting closer to the time for my family to make the trip to see me. Jan and Jenny, from my past, were supposed to come with them, but Mom covered for me when I said that the girl, I was now dating was coming to meet them. Mom tried to remind me that Dawn would share a room with Laura so that Laura would not be given the wrong impression. I had a long talk over my weekly phone call with Mom the Friday before they flew down to catch the ship on that Sunday. I told her that I was grown and that she and Pop would have to realize that I was a drinker now and that Dawn would be staying in my room with me. You could have heard crickets on the other end of the phone.

Dawn had arrived early enough to go with me to meet them at the airport. It was my parents, my younger sister, and my middle sister, her husband, and their two young daughters. They would be taking the seven-day cruise. I introduced them to everyone that I could. I even got to introduce them to the captain at his cocktail party. I made sure they saw everything and did everything they wanted to do. On the ship, one could eat eight separate times a day and finish off with the

59

Midnight Buffet. Pop took gambling lessons, and Mom did wine-tasting—the works. They all attended every show and sat at the captain's table. I had already asked the cast to pick on Pop and my brother-in-law during every show that included audience participation spots. Gerald had brought along their video camera, and he filmed everything. I still have the video today, but now it is on a flash drive. They all still talk about it and also have pictures galore.

A few weeks after my parents came down, Connie and Greg came back on the ship. Connie sat me down and said that they had heard reports that my drinking and carousing were getting out of control. Luckily, it was not affecting my performing, but they had taken a chance on me and wanted to know if I still wanted to continue for another tour when this one was over. She said that I had seven days to think about it, but then she would need my answer. It was so that they could train another guy for my part if I chose to leave. She also said that if I stayed, I would have to straighten up and, in other words, get myself together.

I spoke with Dawn, and I was worried that she would find someone else at college. I was also a little homesick and did not want to spend the holidays on the ship. So, in the end, I decided to leave the ship when my tour was up.

On the night before we pulled into Miami for what would be my last time, Bob, Sandro, and I stayed awake the entire night and watched the lights of Miami come into view. When we docked, we went back to our rooms and gathered our belongings. Besides everything that I had brought with me,

I had added some more clothes and one huge box that was filled to the brim with souvenirs for the family back home. When the customs officer got to me for inspection, he just asked if I had anything to declare, and I told him that everything in the box was what I had acquired over my time on the ship. He opened the top and just said, "Okay," and stamped it "Searched." I could have had another brown paper-wrapped "loaf of bread" in the bottom, and he would have never known. I did not just in case you are wondering.

I had changed my flight plans home to a later date and a different airport. I would be riding with Bob up the coast to Jacksonville, where I would meet Dawn and her roommate and go back to Gainesville. They had an apartment near the University of Florida, where they were going to school at the time. I had arranged this with her roommate without Dawn knowing, so I could surprise her. It worked well, and I stayed with them for a little while before going home.

Chapter 18

After returning home and settling back in, I had to find a job. If I was going to make this long-distance relationship work, I needed to make some money. My middle brother, Mike, was working for a business that made power plants for huge computers. They hired me, and I made the large power cables and would help build the units. I made enough money to fly down to see Dawn or fly her up to stay with me at my parents'. Sometimes, she would pay for her flights. My family really liked Dawn and were pulling for us to work out.

Even though I was not a "practicing catholic," I was still a part of the Knights of Columbus, because of Mom and Pop. I could not become a Knight until I had turned eighteen. My brothers and my brother-in-law, Gerald, were all members. I had been involved with the association ever since I turned thirteen. They have a younger version, called The Squires. One had to be catholic in order to belong. We would take a weekend trip and snow-ski in the winter, and to a lake for a weekend where we would camp and water-ski in the summer. There are four degrees we could achieve in the Knights, but we could not hold an office until we reached fourth degree.

Pop wanted us all to be fourth-degree members. By this time, I was already a third-degree member, and the fourth-degree convention was coming up in Richmond. The fourth degree was the "formal" degree and required wearing a tuxedo for all of the formal events.

I planned for Dawn to fly up for the convention; however, I had more in store than that. We had talked about her moving up to Virginia to finish school, but Ellen, her mother, was not too thrilled about the idea. She said that if Dawn moved to Virginia, she would not finish school. Ellen also said that she would not pay for Dawn's school if she moved.

So, I planned to propose to Dawn when she landed in Richmond. A local radio personality that I knew pulled some strings and got me a limousine to pick her up in. Then, we would drive to a lake I knew in the city, and I would "Pop the Question" there.

It had all gone over without a hitch, and we had a wonderful weekend. My oldest sister even had made her a formal gown to wear. (Oh, yeah—she said, "Yes!" if you were still wondering.)

When she got home, though, things started going south with her and her mother. She started giving Dawn ultimatums about everything, especially things that had to do with us. Eventually, we had plans for us to go to Boston, Massachusetts together for Thanksgiving to see her brother. Her mother, Ellen, made Dawn call me and break things off entirely. Dawn told me that she had found out that she was pregnant, and her mother made her get an abortion. She was also going to pull her out of school and make her go back home and attend a community college there. She was never going to be allowed to contact me ever again, and I had to do the same. To top it all off, Ellen was still expecting me to pay the three-hundred dollars for the ship-to-shore phone call that she had given the go-ahead for in the first place. This had come out of nowhere and devastated me to the core. Dawn was crying, and I was crying. This happened at the end of October, a little more than a month after proposing.

I remember walking out to the backyard and screaming. Pop came outside and asked me what was wrong, and I told him. He asked me if I thought it was true about the baby. I told him that Dawn sounded pressured, and not like herself. He said to give it a few days and try to call her back. I was inconsolable. I left and started walking down the street. Mom sent Gerald after me because he and Sharon had come over. He did his best to calm me down, but like I said, I was inconsolable. For the next few weeks, I was a wreck. I had a tough time functioning.

One night, while I was home with just Mike, I grabbed a steak knife and went into the bathroom but forgot to lock the door. Mike was downstairs, in his room, blasting music. I sat between the bathtub and the toilet. I put my arm on the side of the tub and tried to kill myself. Instead of cutting just my wrist, I ran the knife up my arm from my wrist to my elbow. It was deep enough to bleed, but not so deep as to do enough damage. I just sat there and closed my eyes. I did not know that my brother had come upstairs to see what I was doing.

He had opened the door and found me. He started yelling at me and wrapped my arm in a towel. After running it under the faucet, he saw that the cut was not too deep. He called me an idiot and said that Mom and Pop were going to kill me. He found some gauze and bandaged me up before they got home. He covered for me, but I think it was mainly for himself, and he told them that I caught it on a nail downstairs. They did not find out until years later when I told them.

CHAPTER 19

I had lots of jobs, so I could still try and sing if the opportunity ever presented itself. In 1989, I got a call from a guy who had a part-time band that I had heard of through his son. His son and I went to middle school together. He said that he had heard I was back from the cruise ship and asked me if I was interested in auditioning for a part-time band that needed a male lead singer.

Here was my chance to get back on my feet and stop feeling sorry for myself. I had set up an audition on one of their practice nights. I pulled up to the house where the band leader and drummer, Jim, lived. They practiced in a garage out back. Unbeknownst to me, another guy was there for an audition before me, and he was coming out as I was walking up. We said hello to each other, but nothing more.

When I walked into this cramped space, there was a bass player, Brad; a keyboard player, Walter; a saxophone player, Gary; a guitar player, Paul; and a girl singer. Jim was sitting behind the drums. The girl singer was a good-looking blonde named Dawn. *(Another Dawn! Really?)* They all smiled and welcomed me in. They asked me about myself, including my time on the ship, and if I could play any instruments. Then they had me sing through a few songs. It was not that bad. They were a tight group.

By the end of the audition, Jim had offered me the job and explained the pay, travel, what they wore for shows, and the type of shows we would play for. Now, I was back in the business and could still work another job to make ends meet. Rehearsals were on Thursday nights, and I picked things up fairly quick. They played a variety of music. I listened to about every type, so I knew a lot of the songs already. All of the gear fit in an old box truck, and the rest of us rode in Brad's van.

Our sound man was named Jack. He definitely knew his stuff. He could fix any piece of the equipment because he and Jim were both electricians. The band was called *First Class*. We only played on Friday and Saturday nights, so our travel distance was limited to as far north as Washington, D.C., all of Virginia, and a little bit of the border of North Carolina. I already had all the clothes I would need, so my paycheck mostly went to my car. I still lived at home, so I did not have to pay rent. My old ways and the memory of "Cruise Ship Dawn," as she was remembered by my family, still controlled my actions. She would always be Dawn Marie, my first true love. From then on, I lived life in the *fast lane* 24/7 to try and forget her. I was the master of my own destiny and took advantage of <u>every</u> opportunity that came my way, chemical or personal.

Side story: At one time, I was working for a singing telegram business in the county, and I was also still doing the

Master of Ceremonies act for some local pageants. I was asked to do a pageant in a county just south of where I lived. There would be a rehearsal on a Friday night and the pageant was the next day. The lady who ran the show said I could crash on her sofa Friday night, so I did not have to go all the way home and come all the way back early in the morning. So, my singing telegram boss allowed me to take the business van to carry the PA system I owned down to a high school for the pageant. I also brought a pillow and a blanket. That van saved my life that night. After the rehearsal, I followed the lady and her daughter back to their house. I had taken my shirt and shoes off, but still had on my pants. I laid down on the couch and cut the light off. The next thing I knew, the light had been turned on over my head, and an angry-looking man was nose-to-nose with me. He said, "What in the (blank) are you doing in my house?" Just then, the lady came up behind him and tried to tell him who I was and why I was lying on his couch. The lady had not told her husband that I was going to stay there instead of going all the way back home. Needless to say, and I do not blame him, he was going ballistic! They went into the bedroom and continued their argument in there. Meanwhile, I sat up on the sofa and put my t-shirt back on. I was feeling for my socks and shoes, all the while keeping an eye on their closed bedroom door. I finally was dressed, and I grabbed my coat and ran out of the house and to the van. I could not imagine what that guy thought when he pulled into his driveway and saw a white cargo van with "Balloons and Tunes" written really big on the side. It also had balloons, music notes, and clowns painted on it. It was freezing outside, but I got in that van and locked the doors. I had started the van when the husband started knocking on the driver-side window and telling me to come back inside. I yelled, "That's alright; I'm leaving." I drove straight to the high school and slept in the van. I kept warm under the cargo blankets that I had used to wrap my equipment. I showered in the school the next morning. That was the last pageant I would ever work again. Now, back to the story.

When I was on stage, I was on. Nothing got in the way of me performing. I would do about anything to get a reaction from the crowd, no matter how big or small the crowd was. The girl singer, Dawn, and I came up with all kinds of choreography, and our voices complemented each other. We did have our disagreements, but they were short-lived. Sometimes, she would tell me I was overdoing it and to pull it back. I did not listen to her much, but she did laugh when I did some of the crazy stuff just to get noticed. (And if you are wondering, yes—we had a tryst.) I made quite a few connections and got the band a lot of business because of my entertainment value and stage presence. My cockiness was as prominent as ever, and I even told our agent, while he was standing with a female agent, to move out of the way and take his girlfriend with him; I was getting ready to perform. Did I say I was cocky?

CHAPTER 20

I performed with this group from 1989-1992. In 1992, two things happened that would put a little hiccup in my life. One was <u>great</u>, and one ended up being not so great. I was in a local grocery store when I met Sheri. She was a cashier—and a cute redhead! I had never dated a true redhead before. I will give you a taste of the cockiness. All I was buying was some boxed mac and cheese, and Sheri said, "Is that all?" to which I responded, "No, I need your number, too." She smiled and gave me her number and was at my parents' house the next day.

We started dating, and I became very possessive of her, and she of me. She was eighteen and was graduating soon, and I was twenty-four. I went to Jim and asked if she could come with us to the gigs (jobs), and she could run the light system for us. He was apprehensive, but he agreed.

After she graduated, we talked about moving in together, because her parents would not let us be alone at their house. I made another <u>big</u> mistake and said, "Well, if we were married, we could live together."

We ended up going to the Justice of the Peace for a quicky marriage. We moved into an apartment just across the bridge from my parents. I remember the first meal she "tried" to cook for us. She burnt the pan so bad that the bottom had first turned red and then black. Oh, well; our private life was good.

The end of our relationship happened extremely fast and cost me both financially and emotionally. Sheri had gotten the idea that she was going to be a singer, too. She had a friend that had moved to Nashville, Tennessee and said that she had connections in the music business and wanted Sheri to visit and meet some of the people. She could not go to any more gigs because Jim said that I was starting to hold back in my performances while watching after Sheri. She would dance while doing lights and attracted the wrong kind of attention. It was alright for me to do it, but not for her. I was performing, doing a job. It came close, one night, to making me get in a fight with a young guy in the club for just saying, "We will see you later," as she and I were leaving.

Sheri had auditioned for some country band as their lead singer. I tried to be supportive and went to see them one night. It was a place called Johnny's, just inside the city limits of Richmond. A smokey, little dive that attracted what I, back then, called "Rednecks." She did well, but I did not want to stay. The smoke was killing me. She brought up the Nashville thing again, and I told her that the only way she was going was if I drove her there. So, she set it up with her friend and we would leave early in the morning, right after I had finished performing at a club.

I was going on two hours of sleep and trying to drive. We had gotten about four hours into the trip when I fell asleep at the wheel and went off the road. I pulled my white mustang convertible, my baby, the car that Pop told me not to get behind the wheel of tired, back onto Highway 81 in Pulaski, Virginia. I fish-tailed and spun the car around. It seemed like everything was going in slow-motion. The front of my car hit the guardrail and continued to spin back across the highway and ended up stopping after hitting the opposite guardrail.

Sheri was screaming and holding her head. I was disoriented for a few seconds. This was before airbags, but we both had on seatbelts. Sheri's head was bleeding at her hairline, but I did not have a scratch, just maybe a concussion. I remember this guy coming up to the car. He was young and was wearing a lifeguard shirt. He said, "Are you alright? Can I help you?" He saw Sheri bleeding, and he pulled open his bag and put a compression bandage on her head.

When the troopers, firefighters, and ambulance pulled up, he said that we would be alright now; then, he was gone. I do not remember where he went. The emergency workers even asked where I got the compression bandage. I pointed in the direction the young man went, but he was gone. I seriously think he was an angel.

I was standing outside the passenger side of the car. My car was totaled. There was hardly anything left of the back end. It had been pushed to the back seat, and the car was smoking a little. They took us both to the hospital, where Sheri had to have stitches. I was lying in the next room, and there was only a curtain between us.

Her parents arrived in no time, and I could hear them, in the next room, talking about what and how this had happened. Her dad, a noticeably big and scary Marine Veteran, was very agitated and wanted to know where in the heck I was. He then pulled back the curtain and laid into me verbally. How I had messed-up his daughter's face and her chance at a singing or modeling career. How I was jealous of her contacts in Nashville and how he was going to sue my parents. He said a lot more, but it is unfit to write here. All I could think about was my parents and how I had let them down once again. I was also petrified of them being sued by this raving maniac.

Sheri's parents got us something to eat and a hotel room that was close-by. Sheri did not say much to me, and when we got to the hotel room, her dad said, "You two will take that bed, but keep your clothes on." We were newly married, but I was not going to cross him.

When we got up the next day, we drove to where (what was left of) my car was sitting and retrieved our belongings. I had to pry the suitcases out of the back. That was the first stage of failure. The whole way home, Sheri's parents were trying to reassure me that they were not going to sue my parents, that they were going to sue our insurance company. I thought, *"What's the difference?"* When we arrived home, Sheri and I went back to our apartment, still not talking.

I went to my day job the next day and when I got back, I was greeted with Sheri holding a cat. Her parents had given it to her. They had found it. I was allergic to cats. We'd had cats at my parents' house, but they stayed outside. After less than a week, the apartment was covered in fleas. I'd had enough. Sheri and I were over.

She moved back with her parents, and I was left with the lease and the fleas. I had gotten another car; this time, a clunker—again, thanks to Pop. I went over and picked Sheri up and we went to the courthouse and got an annulment. We had not been married for six months, so it was pretty cut-and-dry. So, when I drove her back home, her dad was waiting for us at the door. I had pulled into the driveway a little bit and Sheri yelled, "STOP!" I slammed on the breaks, and she jumped out. Just then, I saw her dad raise up a rifle and point it in my direction. I was already backing out when I heard the shot, and something hit the top frame of my windshield. It had hit right above my head. He had tried to shoot me! He was an unbelievably bad drunk because of his time in Vietnam, but I never thought that I would get shot at. I did not tell anyone about what happened until now.

I drove straight back to my apartment after stopping to buy flea bombs. I let off four canisters of that stuff and spent the night at my parents'. The very next day, I went to the rental office and told them that I was not renewing my lease and would be out by the end of the month. I returned to my old cocky self with the band, and things kept going right along.

CHAPTER 21

A year or so later, Jim asked me to help him move some furniture down to Florida. I said, "Sure." So, we left early one morning, in the new band truck, for Florida. The closer we got, the more I thought about Dawn Marie. Just wondering where she was, what she was doing, you know, that kind of stuff. The new truck was bigger and a lot better than the old one. On the way down the road, we talked about everything but "The Biz." We had finally made it to Orlando, Florida. We would be staying with Jim's wife's family.

There was an unexpected surprise when we got there—at least for me, that is. Jim had a niece, by marriage, named Angela. She was blonde and a little younger than me and quite a looker. She had a boyfriend named Byron, but she made sure to tell me that they were just dating. It was someone's birthday, if I remember correctly. Angela and I talked for hours. She wanted to know everything about the music business, at least what I had been involved with.

Jim and I were leaving the next day, and Angela told me that she would like to come up and visit. She said that she had talked to Jim, and he said that she could visit that upcoming summer. That was just a few weeks away. When Angela was to arrive at the airport, Jim said that I could take their Ford Probe to pick her up. I got to Jim's house in enough time to not have to rush. Angela's plane was on time, and we drove back to Jim's house. She stayed for the weekend. We did not have any gigs, so I showed her around Richmond and the surrounding counties. We spent a lot of time together.

When I took her to the airport, we kissed, and she promised that she would see me soon. We wore out the phone lines, and one night, she said that she was moving up to Virginia to live with Jim and his family. I was incredibly surprised; however, the next sentence was a bit of a shock. Angela said that she would need her car and wanted me to come down to Orlando and drive her and her car back up to Virginia. I stuttered, but I said I would. Jim gave me money for a bus ticket, and he took me to the bus station at midnight. I would be on that bus for almost twenty-four hours. It was interesting and very tiring, to say the least. Angela came to pick me up, and I would stay at her house for a day, and then we would leave at midnight the next night.

I remember swimming in her family's pool and Byron showing up. He had heard that Angela was leaving and moving to Virginia to be with some singer in a band. He also knew that the singer was swimming in her pool right now. He was trying to get into the house any way he could. Angela, her mother, and father were running interference until I could get in the house and hide somewhere. That was another reason to leave at midnight under the cover of darkness.

I drove all night, only stopping for bathroom breaks and something to eat. I helped move her into Jim's house and was there a lot. It was short-lived though, her staying at Jim's house. Their daughter went to them and said that Angela and I were fooling around in Angela's bedroom. This was not true. I had a lot of respect for Jim. Jim's wife got mad and kicked her out anyway. Her own family. We were not even in the house then. We were sitting on the front porch at the time. Their daughter was not Jim's biological daughter, so her mom indulged her every whim, and she could do no wrong. Angela had found a good paying job, so we found her a studio apartment not too far from her workplace. We had our difficulties, but we were doing alright together.

CHAPTER 22

The band was going through some changes, and Jim was not taking it well. The sax player, Gary, and Dawn, the girl singer, said that they were leaving the band. All the rest of us started looking for their replacements. Years later, I would find out that "Girl Singer Dawn," had passed away.

Jim was the one who found a husband and wife who were interested. Allen and Donna joined the group in early 1992, I believe. Allen could sing, play some horn, I think, and play keyboards. Unfortunately, I made his wife and our new girl singer, Donna, uncomfortable. I was just doing my thing, and she kept telling me to slow down because she really was not into moving like Dawn used to do. But I just kept doing my thing, and I even started bringing my trumpet and playing some tunes with Allen. I was still thinking about doing bigger and better things with my music though. I wanted to be in a full-time band or have my own band, travel more, and have a tour bus. I did say that I was a *dreamer*. The band was still playing every weekend, but it was not the same.

There was a big event coming up that I had always heard Jim talking about. It happened every year. It was called "The

Showcase." It was when our booking agents at East Coat Entertainment would invite their best bands to come and perform a limited set for prospective customers. It would practically run all day with multiple stages. We were chosen to perform a set, and I was ready to shine.

I did not know until we got there that a beach music band from Virginia Beach would be performing later. They were a six-man group with a horn section. They were called *Fat Ammon's Band*. Everyone sang, and some played multiple instruments. Fat Ammon was the original drummer for a high-profile beach music band called *Bill Deal and the Rondels*. They had national hits on the radio back in the day and were big in the Myrtle Beach shag scene on the U.S. East Coast. Don, who was the bass player, and Ammon left that band and started Fat Ammon's Band (FAB) in 1978. They were a full-time band that traveled from Canada to Florida and east of the Mississippi. I remember saying to myself that I was going to be in that band someday.

Our set went very well and had a lot of interest. The guys from FAB had come in by the end of our set and were standing off-stage, watching. When we had finished, I said hello to the guys I had met before. One was their drummer. As we chatted, I told him that I was going to be in their band someday. He laughed and said, "Be careful what you wish for, Chris." After packing up and loading out our equipment, I stayed around to watch them perform. They used choreography, had a huge sound, smoke, and a light show. They even performed their signature "Floor Show." They would do song-skits from The

Blues Brothers, The Supremes, Elvis, and more. They had it down to a science. The Supremes were the best! Three guys would dress in drag and imitate The Supremes, performing a medley of their hits.

After they had finished and were packing up, one of the members, named Lee, who played keyboards, trumpet, trombone, and sang and was also Don's son, walked up to me. Don was now the road manager and ran sound and lights for the band. He also drove their tour bus. Lee introduced himself and asked if we could talk. I said, "Sure," and we went over in the corner. Lee explained that he and Don saw my performance and were wondering if I would be interested in joining the group. He also asked how soon I could leave First Class. You could have knocked me over with a feather. I told Lee that I would be extremely interested, and I would have no problem leaving the other group.

I called Jim that night and told him what had happened and gave my notice. I would finish out the month with First Class while going to any gigs with FAB that I could. I wanted to get the hang of how they operated. I remember my first gig with FAB. It was in Richmond at a night club called Fanny's. They were playing both Friday night and Saturday night.

So, I met up with Lee that Friday at the hotel. We went to his room, and he worked with me on some trumpet parts. I could play the trumpet; however, I was not a trumpet player. They provided me with a shirt that matched theirs. It was common for beach bands to have matching shirts with white, black, or khaki pants and matching shoes.

The first night was incredibly hard. I went back home and could hardly sleep. I was so jacked-up on adrenaline. I had to be back early the next day to do some more practicing with Lee. I also had a ton of lyrics to learn. I spent the next week writing out all the lyrics that Lee did not already have. For my performances, I would put a stack of lyrics on my vocal monitor so that I could see them.

It got easier, but the hard part was about to begin. I performed my last weekend with Jim, and it was hard leaving. He had done so much for me, but I also had to deal with Angela. I signed a contract with FAB and would have to move to Virginia Beach. While I searched for an apartment down there, I lived on the tour bus. It was parked in a warehouse that was part maintenance shop, part rehearsal and recording studio. Angela could not go with me. So, after a very tense and long talk, she moved back to Florida. The warehouse was on 17th Street, about four blocks from the oceanfront. First Class folded not too long after I left.

I did not know how I got to this place in my life. I thought that someone up there was looking out for me; still, I also thought, in my self-centered mind, that it was all me.

CHAPTER 23

I had my pick of females, and this would only cast that net wider. I found an apartment one street over from the shop. It was part of a house that had been divided into four separate units. Mine was the largest, and kind of was laid out in a "U" shape. I was set up for business, and business was booming.

I was in a full-time band that traveled in a fifty-foot Silver Eagle tour bus, which was once previously owned by the rock band KISS. Oh, the stories I am sure those walls could tell. It was brown and silver and held all of our equipment. Inside, it had four sets of bunkbeds, two couches, a television with a VHS player, a sink and microwave, a refrigerator with freezer, and a shower-bathroom combination. There was also a back storage area that held our small road cases and lighting cases along with our clothes bags. Under the bus, we stored the heavier stuff, like our PA system.

We all had specific jobs to do while setting up. We doubled as the road crew. I was in charge of setting up the lights for each performance. The number of lights we used depended on the space we had and the event. We also had both a small and large PA system. I slept in a top bunk because that is where all the new guys were put. It was just big enough for me to lie flat, with about six inches to spare at my head and feet. There was a little shelf above my feet and a small light above my head, and I could almost sit upright. There was also a little curtain that I could pull closed for privacy. One of the bunks was unoccupied because we traveled with seven people. Six on stage and Don at the mixing board.

Since this band was full-time, I did not need another job, which was great. I was close enough to walk to the beach and the store, and to meet the bus when we had to leave. I did not have a car down there, so I had to rely on my bandmates if I needed anything that I could not walk to or have delivered. I had modest furniture; still, two things that I splurged on was a waterbed and futon sofa.

I tried to make myself useful to the band, off-stage as well as on-stage. I was able to design a tour shirt for us to sell at the gigs. They had them before, but they were only one color. The best one I did was six or seven colors, and it was a wolf dressed in a white suit, matching shorts, and sunglasses. He was standing next to a light pole on the boardwalk and spinning a trumpet. We sold a lot of those shirts.

There were pros and cons to this job, just like any other, and it was equal. Some of the pros for me were the constant travel, meeting new people in different states, and going to various places. The pay was unreal at the time, at least to me. We each made $750 bi-weekly, guaranteed, and that was if we played up to five jobs in a two-week period. If we played *over* five jobs in two weeks, we would each make $150 extra, per job, in that two-week period. I really enjoyed playing the outdoor venues and beach festivals.

As I said before, this band was well-known, so we always had a large crowd, which gave me more opportunities to put on more of a show. I would jump up on the speaker stacks while singing—just do my thing. The more I did, the bigger the response. The guitar player at that time, Larry, called me "Stump-Jumper," or "Stump" for short. He said he called me that because I was always jumping on one thing or another during performances. I was told that if Don ever called me that, it was my nickname forever. And he did, so "Stump" it was—just in the band though. It had nothing to do with my physical presence.

However, some of the members were not too keen on all the attention I was getting, and that was one of the cons. It was starting to show with the band leader, who was named Ed, and his nickname was "Eddie-Baby" because he sang the song "Stroking'" and had lots of charisma. The ladies loved him. There was another guy named Curtis, who really put on the charm and had a velvety voice. He sang a lot during our dinner music sets. There was an underlying competition going on that I did not know about until later.

Chapter 24

The road life was difficult on my health as well. I still had not gone to the doctor to get answers about my stomach problems. I really did not think much about it because it could cause me to lose another dream job. Another con was down-time on the tour bus. There were just so many times I could watch the same old movies. Luckily, I had quite a few. We had certain guys who would drive the bus while the others rode shotgun to keep the drivers awake. We would do this in shifts. The bus would literally never stop unless we made it to a truck stop that was close to the next gig. Those truck stops were a saving grace for me. My stomach would not give up, and I always had to go to the bathroom.

One funny story that I can look back on was not funny at the time. Lee was driving and I was riding shotgun. I was more than tired, and I accidentally fell asleep. Don had kind of this sixth sense, and he had woken up and saw me asleep. He grabbed some kind of pan and smacked the shelf that my arm was resting on while striking my knee at the same time. I got a true-blue blessing-out about why I needed to stay awake and that he better not see me do it again. That is one lesson that I learned and never repeated.

If we had to perform in Florida or north of Washington, D.C., we would leave at midnight the night before. It was nothing to have a gig in Florida one night and be playing in Virginia the next. During my first year, we were one of the acts in a Rock and Roll 'Fifties Review Show. The "Master of Ceremonies" was the late Wolfman Jack from the movie *American Graffiti*. The other acts were The Temptations and The Four Tops. We played the first show at the Arthur Ashe Center in Richmond, Virginia, then the next night was at The Norfolk Scope in Tidewater, Virginia. Both were sold-out shows.

On the Fourth of July of my first year, we played on the tarmac at the Farmville, Virginia airport. There was a big stage under what looked like a circus tent. There was a huge crowd and lots of beer trucks, which were a staple at all of the out-door events. During one of my songs, a brunette came up to the front of the stage and reached up and grabbed my pants leg. The stage was a good five-or-so feet off the ground. She motioned for me to lean down, and I did. She asked me if we were staying the night because she wanted to take me home. I could smell the hint of alcohol on her breath and kind of just said, "Okay."

At the end of our show, they were going to shoot off fire-works, so we stayed to watch them. We were standing out-side of our bus after changing, and the same girl found me. She said her name was Leslie. Leslie then handed me a piece of paper with her number on it and said to call her because she and a girlfriend were coming down to the beach and she wanted to see me. I said, "Okay," and my bandmates just shook their heads. The band left that night for Florida.

Leslie lived in Farmville with her brothers. She had a lot of them, and she was the youngest and only girl. Her parents were divorced. One lived nearby and one lived in Colorado.

When she came down to the beach, she called me, and we had just pulled in from a week-long trip. I was tired and told her that I would call her back when I woke up. When I finally woke up that afternoon, I went to meet her at her hotel. We spent the few days that she had at the beach hanging out. We started a relationship and saw each other when I could.

One night, the band was playing at a nightclub near the Richmond airport. My parents had decided to come see us. As we were getting ready to start, who walked in, but Leslie. She was wearing a sundress. She smiled and found a seat near my parents. They did not know each other at the time, but Pop was no fool. On a break, I asked Leslie why and how she was here. She told me that she called our booking agent and found out where we were playing. One of her brothers had lent her his car, and she came to surprise me. That night is when our relationship started. Within a few months, she had moved in with me at the beach, at the end of October of that same year, when we had just gotten back from being out on the road.

I walked back to my apartment, and a few moments later, there was a knock on my door. It was Lee, and he said that he needed to tell me something. I was being let go by the band.

He said that Ammon and Don did not think it was working out and that they were also worried that my health was not doing so well. I was floored. It was like someone had knocked the breath right out of me. He also said that I would stay with the band until the end of November. *What had just happened?* Now I was looking at no job again, and my girlfriend had just moved in with me. Leslie tried to console me, but that was not happening.

CHAPTER 25

After it had sunk in, I started planning on what to do next. Leslie had been a magician's assistant and worked on some big shows that used other performers and large cats. She reached out to a contact, and they were willing to give me a job, but we would have to relocate to Laughlin, Nevada. I sold everything I owned at that time and bought two train tickets to Colorado. We would stay with Leslie's mom and stepfather until the show started rehearsals.

The train ride took two and a half days, and we were sitting in coach. It was all I could afford. I really enjoyed going cross-country on the train. It was December. At night, it was pitch-black outside, and then we would see, in the distance, a clump of Christmas lights. One of the nights, they showed a movie up in the observation car. One of my sisters had made us sandwiches, so we did not have to spend too much money on food. She had even packed us some drinks. The train made many stops, and we could get off if we wanted to.

We got off in Chicago because I wanted to see the terminal. The scenery was beautiful. Most of it was snow-covered.

When we pulled into Denver, we could not leave the train but could see the Rocky Mountains very well.

We soon left Denver and started the climb into the Rockies. It was definitely not for the faint of heart, but I had my nose pressed to the window. A majority of the climb was on sheer cliffs, which made me feel like the train was ready to fall off, into the abyss. On one side of the train was a rock wall; on the other was a drop-off that ended in a river. We were so high up that the river looked like a creek.

When we pulled into our stop in Grand Junction, Colorado, it was nighttime. We were greeted by some of Leslie's relatives who lived there. We stayed a few hours with them before we had to board a bus that would take us to our destination, which was Durango, the next day.

When we got on the bus, I noticed that the roads were snow-covered and there were no guardrails. We were sitting close to the driver, and he was not wasting any time. I thought that my life was over. We pulled into a small western town, at daybreak, called Silverton. It looked like something out of an old west movie. We had time to grab a light breakfast before we were back on the "Terror Trap," but at least I could see death coming.

When we arrived in Durango, we were greeted by Leslie's mom, Susie, and some guy from her work. I will call him Dave. Leslie had not seen her mother in a very long time. We were driven back to Susie and her husband's three-bedroom apartment. Susie and Dave worked together at a local out-door clothing manufacturer. Susie's husband, Ron, worked for the National Parks Service. He never liked me at all. He liked to pick on me because of my catholic upbringing. He would refer to the pope as the Buck-Buck. I never understood nor cared. Susie and Dave dropped us off and went back to work. It was the first time in two and a half days that we had been alone.

When her parents got home, and we were sitting down to eat dinner, Ron just blurted out, "While you are living here, you will not be sleeping in the same bed or room, and that is it." Later, Leslie had a talk with her mom and resolved the issue.

The first thing that I noticed was how much snow they had on the ground. We went driving around, and the houses had snow up to the roofs and only a pathway from their front doors to get out. It was wild. And nothing seemed to stop in the town, either. I was accustomed to having one snow-flake fall and school remaining closed for a week. The only time schools closed there was if there was a water or electrical problem at the school. It snowed for the first seven days we were there without slowing down. It did not even stop for the entire first month. We would not see the roads in town until late April. I turned twenty-five that year. We would only live in Durango for one year exactly, and in that one year, over eighteen feet of snow would hit the ground. It was their worst snowfall in a long time.

CHAPTER 26

That was not the only unforeseen event that happened in 1993. First, I received a call from the show, and they had decided to move the show to South Korea. Nope. Not going there.

Then, my stomach began to hurt worse, and I started to have excruciating cramps that sometimes would double me over. I was constantly running to the bathroom. I practically lived in there. When I finally had enough, I went to the hospital. Mercy Medical Center in Durango. There was nowhere else.

They found me a gastroenterologist. His name was Dr. Gerstenberger. He diagnosed me with Crohn's Disease, an inflammation of the inner lining of the intestine. He immediately started me on the most horrible medicine, called prednisone. It is an anti-inflammatory steroid, and anyone who has ever had the pleasure understands. All it makes you want to do is eat. I gained about one hundred pounds in a short amount of time and was still gaining. My brother Mike was diagnosed with Crohn's when he was sixteen. Some doctors think that it is genetic. I made several trips to the hospital, and the bills were piling up. I had no medical insurance at all.

I got my first job in Durango working at a photo place where visitors would come in and dress up as cowboys and saloon workers and get their pictures taken. It was boring, but I was working. Unfortunately, it was part-time. I would regularly see hot-air balloons fly over the town. Now, that was cool. There really was not much to do in Durango during the winter. However, when spring finally arrived, the pace picked up. People could mountain-bike, and there was whitewater rafting, along with kayaking. It was a big outdoor recreation town. There was also the Durango and Silverton Narrow Gauge Railroad. There was an old steam locomotive with passenger cars that would take scenic trips to the small town of Silverton and come back.

The next event that happened was when I took Leslie to her doctor appointment. She found out that she was pregnant. *Good Lord, what was I going to do now?* The doctor brought me into the room where Leslie was crying. The doctor asked what I wanted to do about it. My parents had tried to instill in me the right values, and I immediately said that I wanted to keep it and that I would marry Leslie.

We both immediately got jobs and started planning. My health was getting worse by the day, and I was working two jobs. One was at McDonald's, and one was delivering flowers. Leslie worked the makeup counter at a pharmacy.

At the end of the summer, I met a hot-air balloon pilot who was interested in starting a balloon business in Durango. She was a redhaired straight-shooter from Buffalo, New York. I told her that I would love to work for her, and she promised to contact me when things were moving forward. Her name was Karen, and she came back to town for a fall festival. It was called "Snowdown." It featured hot-air balloons, large snow sculptures, vendors, and so much more. We had gone down to a micro-brewery and had some beer while a parade was going down Main Street. When we came out to watch, Karen was going by, pulling a trailer with her balloon basket on the back. She yelled at us and told us to come to the park for the balloon glow. We went, and all the balloons were inflated and looked like blinking lights. We made it to Karen's balloon, and she invited us to fly with her the next day for the balloon launch. I had always wondered what it would be like flying in a hot-air balloon, and now it was happening. What an experience! While in flight, Karen talked to me about being her new company's crew chief. I excitedly said I would love to do it. When we landed, we were treated to a traditional Champagne toast. Air Durango was born and started soon after that. Karen bought a house up the mountain from the apartment. We ran flights every morning that we had a booking. Karen got me a real flight suit to wear. I added a Snowdown hat and hiking boots. If I was in the hospital and she had a flight, she had a backup. I could usually see "Kalyx" fly by. Kalyx was the balloon's name. My job was to drive the chase vehicle and set up and break down the balloon for flights.

Karen became part of our family from then on. We would ask her later on to be our child's godmother.

CHAPTER 27

The next chain of events all happened within a month and a half. First, we got married, and my parents came out. Then, our son was born October first, and a week later, I had my first of four Crohn's surgeries. My brother's doctor in Virginia was coordinating my care with Dr. "G" because Dr. "G" had never seen a case this bad before.

After the surgery, they had to leave my wound open. I just had a large bandage taped over stitches that made my wound look like I had a football for a stomach. I wanted to go home, and Leslie wanted me to go home and get things set up and then they would join me. I did not like the idea because I was getting the feeling that she had no intention of going back to Virginia. She relented, and my brother had enough air-miles to get us plane tickets back.

We had to wait a month before I could fly. It was December 18th, exactly one year to the day that we had arrived in Durango. My brother met us at the airport and took us to surprise my parents. Mom and Pop let us live with them in their basement until we were back on our feet and the doctors put me back together. I had to live with a double colostomy for five months after we had returned.

After the surgery that reattached my intestine, I immediately got a job at the Richmond Coliseum as a security guard doing twenty-four-hour security. I worked from eleven o'clock at night to seven o'clock in the morning. I had a great boss, named Earl. I even experienced my first ghost doing that job. It was called the "Whistling Ghost," and would only be experienced in the Spring and Fall. It supposedly was a construction worker who had fallen to his death, while helping build the coliseum.

One day in 1995, I saw that FAB was going to be playing on a stage that was outdoors at the coliseum. The three of us went to see them. They were surprised at my appearance. I was still on the steroids, but a lower dose, and the weight was coming off. I told them to keep in touch with me, and I made sure that they had my number. Not too long after that, we saw them. I received a call from the band asking if I wanted to go back out on the road. I immediately said, "Yes." I started all over again by first looking for an apartment while living on the newer tour bus they had just bought. Same setup, but nicer. It was not long, before I was moving my family down to the beach. The apartment had two bedrooms and one bathroom, and it was big enough for the three of us and was only two blocks from the ocean. This time, we were farther down the beach, mostly away from the touristy section. There was more privacy and less traffic.

Immediately, things started to sour in our marriage. Leslie wanted to work, and she was tired of being alone. I had just come home from being out on the road. The three of us were lying in our bed when Leslie said that she had been invited to a wedding in Baltimore, Maryland, and she was going and taking our son. When I asked who was getting married, she informed me that Dave from Durango had moved to Baltimore and a relative was getting married and he had invited her. She also said that she would be staying at his house to save money. Of course, this started an argument, but she was going, and that was it. I was leaving the following Thursday, and she left for the wedding that Friday. She said that she would be back on Sunday, and so would I. The band returned home in the early morning hours on Sunday. One of my bandmates dropped me off at the apartment, and I went to bed. When I woke up sometime around noon and they were still not home, I started calling. When I finally did reach her, she said that she was staying another night and would be home tomorrow. That started another fight, and I said that I expected her home today.

Here is a side note that I learned in Durango about Dave. Leslie's mother had shown Dave pictures of Leslie and he wanted to meet her if she ever came out to Colorado for a visit. Now, he had moved to Baltimore, and now, Leslie was up there for a wedding. So, after an exceptionally long and intense fight on the phone, she hung up on me. When I tried to call back, no answer. So, I walked down to the laundromat to wash some clothes. When I arrived there, I was alone. While I was getting some change for the machines, two men came in and robbed me of all my change and what other cash I had. Then they proceeded to beat me up for not having more money. I held my own but received a lot of bruises and a black eye.

I am sure that you are saying, "Did you report it to the police?" No, I did not. Virginia Beach, at that time, was in the process of reinventing itself, so the bad element was still in charge. I limped back to the apartment, dirty clothes slung over my shoulder, and tried again to call Leslie. This time she picked up. I told her what had happened and that I needed her home. She asked if I needed to go to the hospital. When I said "No," she said that she would see me tomorrow.

It was a long night. When she finally returned home the next afternoon, we fought again. I started to get this funny feeling when she said that she needed to go for a ride and was taking our son. I told her that she could, but I would put him in the stroller and take him down to the beach while we both cooled off.

Our fights were never physical; that is not how I was raised. Nor have I ever raised my hand to a woman. I will not say that I have not thought about it, though. After about an hour, I came back with the baby. She still insisted that she was going for a ride and was taking our son. She then put him in the car and drove off. While I was pleading with her not to go, she ran over my foot in the process but did not stop. It was starting to get dark, and hours had passed when Leslie finally called. She told me that she was in Farmville (4 hours away) and that she and the baby were not coming back, then hung up.

So, my wife, child, and car were all gone in what seemed like a second. Not to mention my name was the only name on the car. I would say within an hour of her hanging up on me, a Virginia Beach police car was at my apartment, and two police officers were knocking on my door. I answered and they asked me for my name and driver's license. After I gave them my information, they said that I had to come with them to the hospital to be evaluated. *Evaluated for what?* They informed me that Leslie had called them and said that they needed to do a wellness check on me. I had no choice but to go with them. I was put into the back of the police car (at least it was without cuffs), and driven to the hospital. I went through a battery of questions and then released. I had to take a taxi home. I tried to go back to work like nothing had happened, even though I had told the guys. They were sympathetic and tried to keep my mind off of things.

Chapter 28

After that, my life was one big blur, and the thoughts of "Cruise Ship Dawn" were in the back of my mind. I contacted a friend of mine who was a private investigator and gave him the last information I had on her, and he said he would do his best to find her. The next time we spoke, he told me he had tracked her down, and she was still in Florida. He gave me a phone number and said that she was living with her brother. When I had gotten up enough nerve to call her, her brother answered and, at first, was tentative about calling her to the phone, but she answered. Initially, she sounded upset that I had tracked her down, but we had a pleasant conversation.

It was about 1997. I explained that I was planning a trip to Disney with my son, who was now almost five years old. I asked if I could see her while we were there. She said that she would like that. She came to our hotel room one afternoon after she had gotten off from work. She met my son and said that he looked just like me. We talked for a few hours, then she had to leave. I told her that I wanted her to come back with us and that I was ready to buy her plane ticket. She then explained that she was already in a committed relationship, and as much as she would love to come with us, she could not. We promised to keep in touch with each other, no matter what.

After our flight home, I was right back to work, of course, but I had lots of down-time to kill. I filled it with plenty of women and liquor. When I was not performing, I would be at the clubs that were within walking distance because I did not have a car then, which was good because I was usually drunk. I would stumble back to my apartment. Sometimes alone, sometimes not. I did not like being alone. It was very scary. My mind was always playing tricks on me. I started taking Ephedra or Ephedrine, which used to be available over the counter in a bottle until younger kids found out about them. They were actually over-the-counter speed. One pill would keep me up for hours. One time, I took six and did not come down for thirty-six hours. I would ride my new bike any time of the day or night, do push-ups until I could not feel my arms, or watch television and eat around the clock and not gain a pound. I would usually take them when I got home from being on the road.

The band also encountered a huge setback in July of 1996. We had been playing in Emerald Isle, North Carolina on July the second. We stayed in the bus that night and left the next morning, headed to Culpepper, Virginia to play for the Fourth of July. We had to travel down a narrow two-lane road to get out of Emerald Isle. I was sitting on one of the sofas, which was located behind the driver. "Animal," our drummer, was sitting on the steps near where I was sitting next to Don, who was driving. The rest of the guys were still in their bunks. I remember there were trees lining both sides of the road with the occasional house. I then heard Don yell, "Look out!" then, "Hold on!" I saw "Animal" jump up and turn toward the back of the bus, when I then heard a loud crash. The bus turned to the right, and I was thrown into the television shelf and hit my head, then backwards, hitting my side on the shelf under the microwave.

I was on the floor when the bus came to a stop. I looked toward the front and saw nothing but trees all around. We had been in a crash. I checked on Don and "Animal," and they were okay, but I couldn't figure out what had happened or how we would get out of the bus.

The other guys were thrown out of their bunks, and the floor was covered with our belongings. Don and "Animal" were pushing out the front bus windshield. That was the only way we were getting out of the bus. A tree was blocking the bus door, and it would not budge. Eventually, we all made it out. Just before I jumped out, I thought to grab my camera. I always had my camera because I never knew what I might see or who I might meet on the road. Well, it came in handy that day. I took pictures of everything for the insurance, even what was left of the car that had hit us head-on. It was about one hundred feet down the road behind us on the opposite side of the road.

A lady had lost control of her car and crossed over in front of the bus. Her car hit the center of the bus, and the impact had broken the steering column. Don could not steer the bus, and it veered off the road into the trees. Her car spun down the side of the bus and came to a stop. Luckily for her, there was a little food stand right there, and people pulled her out before the car burst into flames.

When the fire department had put the fire out, there was nothing left of the car except for the driver's seat. There were no injuries to anyone in the band except for "Mr. Accident-Prone" yours truly. I was taken to the hospital in the same ambulance as the driver of the car. She was crying, but other than that, noticeably quiet. I ended up in a neck brace with bruised ribs.

When I was taken back to the site of the accident, Don already had a box truck there, and the guys were waiting for the bus to be pulled out of the woods. It took two heavy-duty wreckers pulling at the same time to get the bus out. When it had been positioned on the side of the road, we got to work unloading and loading. We packed the box truck full, and Don's wife, Sandra, had driven down by then and brought their big car, and we piled in. The show must go on, remember.

We made it to our Fourth of July gig with bumps and bruises, but we never lost a step. All the equipment was in working order; however, the bus was out of commission for a while. We had to make do with the truck and Don's car for about six months. The close gigs were not a problem, but the long-distance ones were a pain. We were used to being able to shower, eat, and relax before and after the gigs. Now we were lucky to find a truck stop with showers on our way to the gigs and after. It took what seemed like an eternity to get the bus back, but Don worked on it day and night, and the old girl was back on the road.

Chapter 29

Even though Leslie and I were separated, and then divorced a few years later, I still tried to make as much time as I could to see my son. I had to prove to the court that I could provide for him. I was saving as much as I could of my paychecks.

One day, while out on the road, my bank card was declined. I called the bank and was told that the IRS had put a freeze on my account and emptied it. The band did not take taxes out of our paychecks, and I was not keeping up with it. I paid child support but was not able to keep up my lease on the apartment. So, once again, I moved back home after planning with Don on where I would meet the bus to go on jobs. Mom and Pop tried their hardest to help with meeting to pick up my son, or they would lend me their car if I were home already. It was very tough because most weekends, I was gone, and that was the time I was supposed to get to see my son. Mom and Pop or my younger sister Laura, who was now married, would sometimes bring him to see me perform.

There were some bright spots in the years between 1994 and 1999. The band got to be the opening act for many big-name artists, like, but not limited to: Michael McDonald from the Doobie Brothers, James Brown, Kool and the Gang, K.C. and the Sunshine Band, Eddie Money, Alabama, Maurice Williams, Pam Tillis, Louise Mandrel, Boots Randolph, comedian Sinbad, and Tanya Tucker. We also got to meet pro golfer Jack Nicholas and "Spock" from *Star Trek* Leonard Nimoy, and we were asked to play at the Presidential Inauguration Gala for then-President George H.W. Bush. We got to shake hands with him; his wife, Barbara; Ronald Regan; and future president George W. Bush. They even presented each of us with a medal that had the presidential seal on it and a red, white, and blue ribbon. We would later perform for Barbara Bush's Charity Gala. We did concerts for the Kentucky Derby and the 1996 Olympics. We were also flown to Thule, Greenland to play at an Air Force base there. I designed five more tour shirts, and two of the designs were used on the covers of the two CDs, which we would record in 1996 and 1999. As I said earlier, we were an extremely popular group and had a large following of fans and friends.

Fans came to all the public shows they could. There were shaggers and partiers. They would buy our merchandise. The females would want to have *more* than our merchandise. Friends of the band were just like fans, but got to know the real *us*, not just the image we put forth on the stage. They were families, and they knew our families. They would share in our grief and would bring us a sense of home. There was a couple that started out as regular fans, but became our *number-one* fans. Then, within a short amount of time, they became our "on the road" family. Their names are Faye and Jerry. Even though they lived in the mountains of Virginia, they would come to see us everywhere. Faye would call me or Don and ask where and when the next public gigs were. They would even try to schedule their vacations around our gigs. We were, and, I am blessed to say, still are, friends to this day.

Chapter 30

When 1999 rolled around, I started to think about leaving the road. The miles were getting longer, and the pay was getting smaller. That is just how it was at that time for everyone in the business. I tried doing some one-man performances under the moniker "Chris LoneWolf Craig." I performed as a headliner at our county and state fairs and even recorded my own CD.

One night in December of that year, my life would change for the better. We had always played a Christmas party for Bluefield Regional Medical Center in Bluefield, Virginia every year. We were a hot ticket up there. To me, it was just another night going through the motions. Unbeknownst to me, there was a female that worked for the company who had spent all year long getting ready for this night. I was told, later, that she had even had breast augmentation done just for me.

After getting dressed, I went inside. They had lots of food, and the place was packed as usual. The party was BYOB (or "Bring Your Own Bottle," for the non-drinkers who are reading this). This party would end up being a lot more fun than I could hope for. The girl, who I had mentioned earlier, was sitting at the table behind Don's mixing board. Every night, I would walk up to Don and talk to him before we started, and this night was no different—except for the feeling of being stared at. I was not used to that when I was off the stage. I then heard a female voice say, "Hey." It had come from the girls' table behind Don. I looked over, smiled, and said, "Hey," back. They all smiled.

However, after our first set, I went back over to Don to ask about something, and one of the girls said, "Hey, Chris, come here." I walked over to the table. There were about five of them, all dressed to the nines. One of them asked if I danced, and I explained that I never asked anyone to dance, for fear that I might make someone else upset by not dancing with them. I always waited to be asked. One of the girls then jumped up and said, "Let's dance!" So, we did. She introduced herself as Beth Ann. She said that all the girls worked part-time at the hospital's fitness center, including herself. I could definitely tell. She was extremely attractive. Short, wavy, blonde hair and a tight, little, black dress and heels. She was explaining that one of her friends really wanted to get to know me better. When I looked over at the table, all eyes were on us.

We danced and talked during my whole break. The same happened on my second break. Before our third and final set of the night started, I told Beth Ann that we were going to do our "Floor Show," and I would need her help. She tentatively said, "Okay." Our "Floor Show" music and introduction started, and the crowd went wild. One of the skits was Elvis, and I prided myself on the job I did. I had the jumpsuit, wig, sunglasses, and scarf. People said that I even sounded like him. That was a huge compliment. I was making sure that Beth Ann was paying attention when I started singing "Love Me Tender."

At a certain part of the song, I called Beth Ann up to the stage, wiped my forehead with the scarf, and placed it around her neck, then proceeded with the show. I would later be told that her friend was livid, and the rest of the group was shocked. You see, Beth Ann was the one who did not want to go to the party that night. She knew nothing about me and little about the band besides what she had been told. Beth Ann was a pre-kindergarten teacher at the time and shared a room with the friend who was in love with me. Her friends had convinced her to go and even brought her an outfit to wear. At the dance, it was her job to talk to me about her friend's intentions. Still, I left with Beth Ann's number.

It was about a week later that I called her. She was surprised to hear from me and also explained the plan that was supposed to happen that night. I told her that I was leaving the band at the end of January and had applied for a job at a cable company that my brother Charlie worked for. During that phone call, we found out that we had a lot in common. Beth Ann was divorced and had a little girl six months older than my son.

We did not see each other again until she made the drive down to my apartment that following February, but we burned up the phone lines. We would take turns driving to see each other. She came down in April for a teaching interview and said that if God found her a job, our meaningful relationship was meant to be. I helped set up the interview, and she got the job.

After a five-month long-distance courtship, we were married on May 12, 2000. It was Mother's Day weekend. We got married, found an apartment, and made plans for her and her daughter, Katie, to move to Chesterfield County. We did not tell anyone our plans. I had met her parents, Artie and Pat, the first time that I came up to see her. Her dad knew of the band and had heard them play prior to me joining. I even remember playing at the golf course for a private function where their house was located. They liked the music we performed, especially the beach music. However, Beth Ann's mother, Pat, was a tough cookie and was skeptical of me. She was very protective of her baby and, especially, her baby's baby. They were always together.

I also got to meet one of her brothers, who is named Brad. He is funny and, at the time, was into rap and R&B music. He has a little girl, also, named Leandra Beth. She was named after Brad's sister. Leandra is three years older than Katie. Brad and Beth Ann are awfully close. They had both endured failed marriages and looked out for each other and leaned on each other for strength. When we had decided to get married, Beth Ann and I knew that it would be hard on her mother, but it was just as hard on Katie. I had come up the weekend that she was moving to help and drive the rental truck back while she would follow behind with Katie.

CHAPTER 31

It was Memorial Day Weekend. I had the marriage license in an envelope that was behind my back, and we were standing in Beth's kitchen when we broke the news.

Beth Ann's dad was happy for us, but her mom, on the other hand, reluctantly just said, "Congratulations." I then handed her mom the envelope and said, "Here's your insurance policy." It was a bad attempt to lighten the mood. To say Katie was upset is an understatement. *Who was this guy that married her mother, but more importantly, was taking her away from her Maw-Maw?* Brad ended up getting married the year after we did, to an incredibly talented and funny lady named Renee.

Our first hours together were not how we wanted to start our married life. The truck was packed, and we were off. About two miles later, we were on the side of the road. The rental truck had broken down. Geez! The good thing was we were not too far from her parents' house. The sad thing was that it was Memorial Day Weekend, and they could not fix the truck or get us a new one until the following Monday. So, we went back to her parents' house and stayed there, and the truck was towed back to the rental company.

It was a tense weekend; however, we made the best of it. Come Monday, the rental company called and said that they did not have another truck available, so I let them have a piece of my mind. After that, the management came up with the idea that they would tow the packed truck "as-is" to their service center in Richmond. They would fix it there, and then I could pick it up and drive it to our new apartment to unload. We did not have to pay for any of the rental.

We had found a three-bedroom apartment that gave a discount to county teachers and was in the town of Chester, where we wanted to live. Chester is a small area within Chesterfield County. We would both have a little bit of a drive to work, but we made it happen. Our first year together was a little on the tough side with the coordination of pick-ups and drop-offs for the kids' visitations. We were both in the same boat; our ex-partners were making it extremely hard to be civilized human beings, but we had decided to be the bigger people. We would both end up going to court many times over custody and child support. It would get worse before getting better.

Close to Thanksgiving of that same year, Beth Ann and I were standing in our kitchen when the phone rang, and I answered it. It was someone in my family. I cannot remember who it was, but what they told me brought me to my knees. My oldest brother, Charlie, had been diagnosed with bladder cancer. This cut me to the core.

Charlie and I worked together at the cable company, and our desks were situated in a way that we could see each other, even though we worked in different departments. Charlie was born on Valentine's Day in 1959. As I stated earlier, he was born with a birth defect called "Spina Bifida." The doctors really did not think he would live through the night. Then they said a week. Then, a month went by.

Charlie was an overcomer, and I looked up to him. He played football when he was young, was in the Cub Scouts, played wheelchair basketball, and played the guitar. He was also ranked top in the state for shooting pool and for Karate. He taught me how to show people with disabilities the respect they deserved and never be afraid to help them.

When I turned sixteen, I started to volunteer with the Virginia Special Olympics. I would also DJ all of their dances for thirty years. He loved the fact that I was a singer in a band and would show up to as many of my performances as possible. When he did, I always made sure that either he was in the wings of the stage or up front, so that he was able to see. I even talked him into going to sing karaoke from time to time. Charlie and I considered ourselves the "Black Sheep" of the family. We were the "Wild Ones." He was always my number-one fan. My love for him was immeasurable.

On February 9th, just nine days shy of his forty-second birthday, he passed away. He was not a big church goer, but I do not wonder if he is in heaven. I know he is. He was a friend to everyone, and no one had a bad thing to say about him. He never sought pity and was respected for that. Early on the morning of his passing, I had woken up and told Beth Ann that we had to go to the hospital. We got Katie off to school and headed that way.

We were walking down the hallway to his room as the hospice nurse was leaving. I knew the look she had on her face. I remember seeing it on the face of the nurse when Paw-Paw Craig had passed. When we got to the room, Pop was alone and standing by Charlie's bed. Pop was not much for crying, but he was crying in his own way. I did not know what to say. All I remember of that exact moment was holding my wife's hand, and hearing Pop say, "He is gone. He called me over to his bed, said that he loved me, and took one last breath." Mom had gone downstairs to get some coffee.

I believe that was the way God wanted it to happen. My Mom was all alone when he was born, because men were not allowed to be in the delivery room back then. Pop always jumped when we tried to wake him up. When we were kids, we were told that it was because when Charlie was born, the nurse came running out to get Pop. He was asleep, and she had startled him awake. So, I am glad Pop was with him at the end. Charlie had lived with Mom and Pop for a substantial portion of his life, except for when he tried being married. He was the only child left at home.

Pop's mother, whom we called "Granny Craig," was also living with them. They were caregivers for a long time. They asked us kids to pick out where in the mausoleum he would be placed and what he should be wearing. I said that he should be placed at a very top spot because he spent his entire life with people having to look down at him, so from now on, they would have to look up. Everyone agreed. Pop said that he wanted Charlie buried in his Knights of Columbus Fourth Degree Regalia. I told Pop, "That was not who Charlie was. He should be wearing clothes that he always wore. What his friends and co-workers would remember, not a tuxedo." He agreed, and Charlie was buried wearing his leather vest, jeans, and a flannel-print shirt.

There was a large crowd of all diverse types of people at his funeral. Bikers to businessmen. On his mausoleum name-plate were words from his favorite Lynyrd Skynyrd song, "Free Bird." It says, "Free As A Bird Now." Rest in Peace, Charlie. Until we are able to act up together again.

CHAPTER 32

Not too long after that, I stopped working at the cable company. I was having a tough time with seeing his empty desk. I tried moving to another desk, but I still had to pass his old desk on the way to the breakroom.

In the beginning of March 2002, my health was rearing its ugly head again, and I was having to deal with an unbelievably bad Crohn's flare-up. I was in and out of the hospital while still trying to keep working. Beth Ann was pregnant with our first child together, and the nurses would wheel me downstairs to her appointments if I was still in the hospital, which I usually was. Beth still jokes that her doctor and nurses would all fawn over me and make sure that I was comfortable while she was lying right there on the exam table. I beat my wife to the punch and had my third Crohn's surgery.

Not too long after I was out of the hospital, Beth Ann and I were blessed with a handsome son, and I got to be there. We named him Jacob Lee. His middle name came from the shared middle names of both of our fathers and my brother Charlie. Jacob would be the piece that closed our family circle.

We were still enduring court battles with our exes over custody and child support. I needed to get back to work as soon as possible. After talking to Beth Ann and my doctors about it, I accepted a job at a middle school as a tutor monitor. It was a fancy way of saying that I ran in-school detention. I no longer had the long, permed hair and manicured beard. My hair had relocated somewhere else, so I cut it all off. I would find out later down the road that it had found a home in my ears and on my back. My "singer good looks" no longer meant as much to me. I was now a nine-to-five worker. I had weekends and the summer off, which was a welcome change. It was a hard adjustment for me, though.

Somehow, that job was the start of me wanting to go into law enforcement. I had no experience but always admired the people who wore the badge, and I wanted to "protect and serve." To get my feet wet after working at the school for a few years, I applied for a job with the Virginia Department of Juvenile Justice, or DJJ. I was accepted and started my training. I graduated at the top of my class and was given a choice of working days or nights. I chose days. I would work from five fifteen in the morning to five thirty that evening on a swing shift. It was three days on and two off. Where I worked was called the Reception and Diagnostic Center. It was the first place the juveniles would be held after being sentenced. They would stay there for anywhere between thirty and forty-five days, just to get them acclimated to prison life. I would fight at least once a day, and the stories I could tell you would either rip your heart out, make you furious, or make you shake with laughter. All-in-all, it was sad to hear the stories and hear them cry for their mothers. I never heard anyone talk or cry for their fathers because a large majority were there because of the lack of one.

I am not judging. There is only one judge, and I am not Him. It did make me want to be in my kids' lives more and appreciate the time that I did have with them. Imagine having to take care of a thirteen-year-old male that was incarcerated for three counts of strong-armed robbery with a shotgun. That kid did not look strong enough to hold a shotgun. How about a Latino gangbanger, which was part of one of the worst gangs in the U.S., threating to kill you if you looked at him wrong? It was a daily struggle. By law, we did not carry any handcuffs or weapons. We only had keys and a uniform with a badge. I was interested in learning all I could about gangs and was even being considered, by the state, to join the Virginia Gang Task Force, with the help of my training sergeant, Sullivan. That was after I was able to decode two messages that were being passed between some gang members in a unit.

However, a spot opened up for me to apply at the Chesterfield County Sheriff's Department first. It was the chance for which I was waiting. It was now 2006, and I had just turned forty. Beth Ann and I questioned if I could make it. After my application was accepted, I was required to run an obstacle course and complete a one-and-a-half-mile run within a certain time. Did I mention *run*? I had not run since the ninth grade, much less a complete mile and a half. I was not prepared, but I made it, and I became a sworn peace officer. I would say the most memorable part of the training was getting pepper-sprayed. That was the worst! Badge, gun, and the honor, the whole nine yards, was bestowed upon me after taking my oath on December 21st, 2006.

The first thing I did was sit my wife and our three kids down around the kitchen table of the first house we would own. I took out my service sidearm, unloaded it, took it apart, put it back together, and placed it in the locked position. I then let each one of them hold it for as long as they wanted and ask me questions. Beth Ann held it for about two seconds. After we were done, I reloaded it and said that no one was to ever touch the gun again. I then locked it in my lock box.

I was put on the night shift, which most new officers were, and worked in the jail. The sheriff's department was responsible for staffing the jail, court security, and transportation of inmates. Unlike police departments, we were considered "Constitutional Officers," which meant we could travel to different jurisdictions and still carry a weapon as long as we had our department I.D. and badge with us and maintained all of our law enforcement powers.

I did work shifts in the courts, which was cool until I had to cuff someone I knew, but I just did my job and not let it interfere. In some circumstances, it actually helped that I knew them. For instance, my supervising sergeant gave me the nickname "The Inmate Whisperer." He would call me over the radio if there was a rowdy inmate that was being brought in or acting up in the intake unit. He said that I used my communications skills in a way that could calm down anyone. We had our share of officers that wanted to fight at any time, but I tried to treat everyone with respect and dignity.

CHAPTER 33

Yet again, the Crohn's monster came to get me. I had my fourth surgery, and after that, I was missing about eleven feet of my intestine. My appendix was also gone. I could not return to the force in a reasonable amount of time for the sheriff, and I was given an ultimatum. Either return to work sooner than the doctors wanted me to, resign my position with hire-back status, or they were going to let me go. I took the only choice I thought I had and resigned my position. We as parents were now financially strapped. I had to apply for disability, and it took almost three years and a lawyer to be accepted. Yet, this, I would come to understand later, was another "God Thing" in our lives.

The kids wanted a dog awfully bad, so in December of 2010, we rescued a black-and-white Australian Shepherd. Her name was Jersey Girl, but we settled on Jersey. She was leery of me at first because a male figure had abused her, but after two days and a whole lot of treats, we were best friends. She slept at the foot of our bed or with the kids and was smart as a whip.

In that same year, I helped start a "sea shanty group." An a cappella trio with a couple of friends, not too long before

I started with the sheriff's department. We would re-enact as Rev-war sailors, pirates, Civil War soldiers and sailors, World War II sailors, and Old English carolers at Christmas. We recorded four CDs of the different music we performed and sold them wherever we went. They were even online. We did very well, and our music was sold all over the world. We were not rich by any means, but it sure was fun.

In 2011, we were singing as pirates at a gala in Norfolk, Virginia, when, after we had finished, I noticed that the left side of my neck was swollen up to the size of a tennis ball. It was right under my jaw. I thought it was just a swollen gland. It had happened sometimes on the road. This time, however, the swelling was not going down, no matter what I did. Hot washcloths, ice—nothing. So, I went to my primary care doctor, where he looked at it and did a biopsy, which came back inconclusive. He then sent me to a specialist, an Ear, Nose, and Throat doctor. This doctor took another biopsy, but said that he had been in practice for thirty years and this did not look like cancer.

The results came back on my birthday, March 31st of 2011, my forty-second birthday. *"Happy Birthday; You Have Cancer!"* It was time to see what I was truly made of as a husband, as a father, and as a man. It did not matter how much money we had or did not have or how much I volunteered with the Special Olympics, helped Beth Ann at school, or supported the kids in their activities, or how successful I had been as a singer. It was time to pay up! I was diagnosed with throat cancer, along with squamous cell carcinoma. It was at the beginning of Stage IV, but had not metastasized yet. I felt like a wrecking ball had hit me. I made the doctor repeat himself, and, after he did, he said that he was going to schedule an endoscopy and look down my throat. So many things went through my mind at that moment. The first thought was, *"I am going to die."* The second was, *"How am I going to tell Beth Ann?"*

I waited until she had finished her school day to tell her. I thought it would be better to tell her at school. That was the dumbest idea ever. When I told her, we were walking out of the building, and she let out a blood-curdling scream. It just echoed. We finally got outside, and I made her look at me in the eyes. Her eyes were watery, and I said, "This, changes nothing! I can beat this!" I did not have any time for cancer because I had so much more to do and live for.

The next thing we did was talk to three doctors in a hospital office. They sat across the table from us and said, "You are going to die, and I needed to start getting my affairs in order."

After they had said what they had wanted to say, I spoke up and said, "The time for talk is over; let us get on with it!"

The ENT doctor performed the endoscopy and removed my left tonsil. It was completely compromised, but he left the right one because he said that I barely had one and the insurance would not pay for both if the right one was viable. What a crock! It was the size of a quarter. What could it be good for, besides flapping when I breathed in and out? Viable, my Aunt Fanny!

The mass was pushing on my carotid artery and diminishing the blood flow to my brain from my heart. After the procedure was over, I went through a battery of pre-screening tests, and then the knots in our stomachs had let up a little. The doctors started the most aggressive treatment I could undergo. Five days a week for seven weeks, I had to lie flat on an x-ray-type table with my head locked in place by a white, plastic-mesh face mask. The first time I went in, they made this face mask that formed to the contours of my face and head. It would lock to the table to keep me from moving my head. I even received my first tattoo. They tattooed a dot on my chest as a reference point so that the radiation would be given in the exact same spot every time. I was given radiation for fifteen minutes directly on my neck. The radiation started the beginning of May 2011 and was finished on June 24th.

There was a bell on the wall just outside of the room. When I had finished my treatments fully, I got to ring that bell. I rang it long and hard, with some help from my son Jacob. I also was given three bouts of chemotherapy. One in the beginning of the radiation treatments, one in the middle, and one at the end.

CHAPTER 34

After a few weeks of the treatments, I started going downhill. I was getting extremely sick and had to have a stomach tube put in twice. This was because I could not swallow very well anymore. The skin on my neck was being burnt to a crisp. I had to have a central line put in my neck to be given IV medicines for pain management and nausea, among other things. Every time they changed the dressing on my neck, layers of skin would come off. Imagine, if you can, the worst sunburn you have ever had, times ten, then have someone pull tape off that spot every other day. That might come close to how it felt. I still have scars from that and the radiation. The radiation even burnt the opposite side of my neck as well. I'm not trying to be so graphic, but throwing up became second nature.

After the scar tissue had built up so bad on the inside of my neck, and Beth Ann and I had raised enough cane. They put a power port in my chest. It had to be surgically put under my skin on the left side of my chest. Then the tubes were put into my veins, then the incision was closed up. They had to do this because my veins were no longer usable and would collapse if they tried to put an IV in any of them. But with the port, they could start an IV, take blood, and give me pain medication, all in that one device without having to stick me multiple times. It can stay in forever.

Those chemicals were horrible. My sweet, beautiful, first-grade teacher of a wife had to be given a crash course in nursing and had to take a leave of absence from school so she could take care of me at home. It was at the worst possible part of the year, the last month of school. It tore her to pieces having to leave those kids after giving them a year of instruction and not being able to see them to the end.

It was twenty-four-hour, seven-days-a-week care—not only of me, but she also had to take care of our kids. Luckily for her, I had to be admitted to the hospital several times. It was my second home. I even spent two months there at one time. I was rapidly losing weight because of not being able to keep anything down. I survived off of protein shakes that were poured into my stomach tube. Whenever I was at home, Beth Ann not only had to crush up all my pills because they had to be put in through the stomach tube, but I had this little machine that clipped to an IV pole. It would manually push the protein shakes through the tube from a bag that she had to fill with protein shake liquid so I could be left alone at night to try and sleep. At times, I also had an oxygen machine to help me breathe or make me take breaths because of being so weak.

To top it all off, Katie, our oldest, was graduating from high school and I could not attend because I was in the hospital again. However, after the ceremony, someone brought her to the hospital, and she came up in her cap and gown to see me. When she got off the elevator, everyone started to clap for her. It was a bright spot in a dark time. Then …

On the night of June 2nd, I had been admitted to the hospital again. I was on the second floor in the cancer wing. In the latter days of my treatments, I could hardly move on my own, much less get up to use the bathroom without calling for help. I was getting violently sick in a trashcan that was always by the side of my hospital bed. For some reason, I made myself get up out of bed. I kicked the trashcan up against the wall. I shuffled over to the wall and put my hands up on it as far as I could. I was straddling the trashcan and had put my forehead on the wall while still continuing to get sick. I then started to pray. I did something that I had never done before. I tried talking to God. I remember it like it was yesterday. I said:

> *"God, I know that I have hardly ever tried talking to You, and it was for something that I really did not need anyway, but You are the only one that I think can help me now. I'm not strong enough to fight this on my own. I tried to put on a strong face in front of everyone, but I can't do this anymore. I need to put it all in Your hands, and if You say that this is it, I'm fine with that, but if this isn't the end, then please show me the way. Whatever You say goes. Please help me, Lord. I know that You won't give us anything that we can't handle. I turn my life over to You and ask*

for Your grace and help. My life is Yours, as it's
always been; I was just too blind and deaf to
understand."

At that moment, an indescribable calm washed over me.
I could feel it start at my fingers and flow all the way down
through the floor, like a <u>huge</u> wave. I stopped getting sick,
turned toward my bed, took two real steps, not shuffling steps,
and laid down in my bed with all the tubes and wires and
actually slept. That was something that I had not been able
to do for a long time.

When I woke up the next morning, Beth Ann was there.
She said that I looked different, a lot more peaceful while I
was sleeping. I told her what had happened the night before.
She immediately pulled out my laptop and showed me how
to find our local Christian radio station on it. That is when
I heard about a new Christian group at that time called *For
King and Country*. They were playing a new song from their
debut CD called "The Proof of Your Love." It really spoke to
me in a way that I could understand. Through music. Beth
Ann looked at me and said, "There is your answer. God's
affirming His love for you." That was the turning point in my
life. From then on, things seemed to progress for the better.

When they gave me my follow-up PET scan, all of the
cancer was gone. That was only a month after my last treatment. The doctors told me that I would be able to talk with
some therapy, and in time, it would come back; however, they
could not say the same for my singing. They said that part

was over, and they said they were sorry. They also said that I had fought and won and should be happy with that. Still, I was not satisfied with that. God had given me this wonderful gift of a singing voice, and I had wasted it. I <u>was</u> going to sing again!

I started trying to sing four months after my last treatment. I was not even talking and swallowing too well then, but I was singing. Granted, I am not as strong as I once was, but if God restores my singing voice just like He has done with my swallowing and my talking, His will be done.

Chapter 35

During Christmas 2011, I started making good on my promise to God. A very dear friend of Beth Ann, Gina, invited Beth Ann and our son, Jacob, to see her kids in their church Christmas program. Jacob was the same age as her daughter, and her son and Jacob were friends. The two of them had such a wonderful time at the program that we decided to go as a family to the Christmas Eve service. When we arrived, Gina had saved us seats in the second row. No lying—I was sweating from sitting so close. I thought it was too close for comfort. But as the choir started singing, a feeling of belonging swept over me, and I knew we were in the right place for us all. And as if things could not get any better, Jacob wanted to go to the New Year's Eve service with Beth Ann and our daughter, Katie. There were two young ladies that got baptized that night. Jacob looked up at his mother and said, "Mommy, I want to do that." And on February 5th of 2012, Jacob was baptized and saved, and so was his dad.

CHAPTER 36

Since then, things have been a rollercoaster of trials and tests. I am guessing that Satan did not like losing his grip on me. Within the next two years, because of my cancer treatments, I began to have seizures. Our niece Leandra was marrying a nice youth pastor named Bryson, and I was supposed to DJ their wedding reception. However, I had started to feel bad again and was hospitalized. I did not know it, but Bryson and Leandra had a backup plan in case this happened, but I was sure that I would be out by the wedding. Unfortunately, I was still in the hospital, and Jacob and Katie were in the wedding party, so Beth Ann left the hospital to drive up to West Virginia for the wedding.

Beth Ann had gotten to Bedford, Virginia, which is about halfway to where she was going, and her phone rang. It was my doctor at the hospital, and he asked where she was. Beth Ann told him that she was driving. He said that she had better turn around and come straight back to the hospital because they were losing me. She almost ran off the road. She called her mother to come and meet her. I had already had three strokes and six seizures. I had then slipped into a coma. I was placed in the Neuro ICU. I was breathing on my own, but would not wake up. Beth Ann had come back and stayed by my bedside. She even had to sign the papers concerning what our wishes were if things got any worse or if I would not wake up. The doctors told her that if I was lucky, I might wake up in around six weeks. I had a lot of pressure on my brain.

Beth Ann had noticed a very dark presence in my room, and she was afraid. The doctors were even turning mean. The lights could not make my room any brighter, so she placed a call to the church that we were attending at the time, and prayer warriors started showing up. One of her best friends, Cheryl, even came and slept in the ICU waiting room with her overnight. One of the prayer warriors was Chuck. He and his wife, Deborah, both have the gift of intercession. Beth would tell me later that Chuck had prayed the darkness out of my room.

Three and a half days after my coma began, I started to open my eyes. The first thing I remember was how very bright it was, but I had not opened my eyes yet. Then I opened my eyes, and the first person I saw was Beth Ann. She told me that the first thing I said to her was, "Your teeth are so bright; it is hurting my eyes." The doctors and nurses were coming in, and they were asking me all kinds of questions, like who the president was, did I know what had happened to me, you know—things like that.

Beth Ann and I do have some humorous things we like to look back on that I would like to share, with her permission. I feel like we all need to find some humor in everything possible. One story was when the doctor asked me if I was married. I said, "Yes."

Then he said, "Is she in the room?" He asked me to point at her.

I looked around and pointed at a pretty, blonde, young nurse and said, "There she is."

Beth Ann was standing right next to my head. I was lucky that Beth Ann did not put me back into a coma.

Then the doctor asked me if I had any children.

I replied, "Yes."

He then asked me, "What are their names?"

I said, "Jacob, then my older son and … Tabuka."

Now, when Katie acts up, I will call her Tabuka!

Something else that I was having trouble with when I woke up was my vision. Soccer was on my television, and Beth Ann said that I was watching the screen with a funny look on my face. She asked me what was wrong, and I said, "Look! They are playing double soccer!" There were two soccer balls on the field. The doctors called what put me in the coma "P.R.E.S." It stands for (are you ready?) Posterior Reversible Encephalopathy Syndrome. It is a disorder of acute onset neurological symptoms due to reversible subcortical vasogenic brain oedema. Boy, is that a mouthful. The most common symptoms are seizures and headaches. So, I now have seizure disorder along with orthostatic hypotension, which means that when I stand up too quick or stretch too hard, my body does not regulate my blood pressure fast enough, and I am prone to passing out. It is usually accompanied by staring and losing control of my limbs. I used to fall quite often, but over time, it has gotten better with medication.

Oh, and since I mentioned medication: I was having to take a total of sixteen pills, three times a day. I had also been informed that I had a "basil brain bleed." There is still a "footprint" of where it was. It does not bleed anymore, but it is deep within my brain and will show up every time I have an x-ray or MRI. With the combination of everything I medically have wrong with me, it has caused some brain damage. I had to spend three months in an assisted living facility, where I had to undergo physical therapy to learn how to talk and swallow again.

Chapter 37

I have been hospitalized many times, and my faith has been truly tested. I came to the realization that I had become dependent on pain killers. It had started way back when I was first diagnosed with Crohn's Disease, and just continued to get worse with each new medical problem or surgery. There were times that I wore a pain patch. Once, while I was sitting in a chair watching the kids play, I passed out. I also was in the hospital and started hallucinating that a nurse was getting ready to over-dose me. After that, Beth Ann came to me one day and told me that she was keeping count of my pain pills and that if I continued on this track, she would have no choice but to leave me.

That is when I voluntarily checked myself into a psychiatric ward for treatment of depression, anxiety, and drug abuse. On October 1st of 2013, I again had a <u>real</u> heart-to-heart with God, and as He always has been, He was with me. It was the twentieth anniversary of my Crohn's diagnosis and the twentieth birthday of my estranged, oldest son. There was a hole that I could not get out of. So, I went to my room alone and asked for God's help, yet again.

The first thing that I heard was, "Look up. That is the only way out of a hole!" I then asked God to show me how to know Him better. And in his undying grace, He gave me the words to a song right then and there. He was speaking to me in the only way I could understand—music. His message was coming so fast that I grabbed a pencil and my journal and laid down on the bathroom floor, which was in my room, and wrote the song "Show Me How To Know You." Within two hours, the song was done, along with the melody.

Chapter 38

I was at peace enough to sleep and continue my treatment. I was released after seven days. And have only used pain medicine when and how I needed it. I was back at church with a zeal that no one expected. I was even trying to use my "gift" to praise God's name, the way it was intended to be used.

After being released from the doctors and labeled "cancer-free," Satan came along again, and we had a falling out with our church at that time. It was the start of a new season for us, I guess. Beth Ann still keeps in touch with the "sisters" that she had while we were attendees there. Cheryl and Kelly helped Beth Ann keep her sanity in check, as Beth Ann did for them in return. We started watching Blue Ridge Church in Christiansburg, Virginia on the computer. It is a church that our daughter Katie goes to. We became very in-tune with it. The lead pastor, Scott, and assistant, Matt, are great, and we loved the worship band and music. We did not want to be "religiously lost" anymore. I had quit being on disability and returned to the workforce as an instructional assistant with special needs students at the high school, the same high school that all our children would eventually graduate from.

Jacob came into our room one day and told us that he had a dream that we had gotten another dog to keep Jersey company. The dog was white, with black spots and a tail, and we called her Lilli. I went to my laptop and found a puppy that fit all the criteria, even the name. I told Beth Ann, and she said that the Lord was speaking to us. So, we rescued Lilli, and now we had two dogs. **God did it again!**

Now, I am always ready for whatever comes next, or at least I thought I was, and it came at me alright. Both of my parents' health had been on the decline for what seemed like years. On New Year's Eve, 2019, I lost my mother. Then, on January 26th, 2020, my father could not live without the love of his life anymore, and he passed away. My parents had six kids, fifteen grandchildren, and fifteen great-grandchildren.

When my brother passed, our family drifted apart. No more family get-togethers, no more family beach trips, no more anything. My parents tried to keep the peace, but after they had passed, our family was broken into what seemed like two teams. My parents had made our youngest sister, Laura, the executor of their estate. That did not sit well with some of my siblings. Laura was with Mom and Pop constantly, up until the very end. She would drive them wherever they needed to go when they could not drive anymore. She took them to doctors' appointments, the grocery store, everything. My sister Sharon and I would fill in the gaps. Pop would call me if the cable went out or he could not get his remote to work. Looking back now, I wish I would have had more time.

I know Sharon and Laura do as well. It is said that "Hindsight is 20/20."

Also, in 2020, COVID hit, and my doctors told me that I would have to get vaccinated because of my low immune system levels. However, before I could get my first shot, I was hospitalized with COVID twice. I was in the hospital for a month each time. But with God, the "Ultimate Repairman," and with "*For King and County*" playing on my computer, I made it through.

I prayed for a long time to the Lord as to what to do next, and He came through, as usual. I looked at my wife, Beth Ann, and I told her that I thought we should move closer to our kids, her brother Brad's family, which now included a daughter named Hannah, and her parents. God then provided in a big way! Our house sold in a day, we both had jobs soon after, and then He found us a brand-new house that was just built where we wanted to live. There was even a rainbow over the house when we signed the papers and moved in. He even provided us with faith-based realtors and loan officer. We did not even have to look for a church, because Blue Ridge Church was already welcoming us into their family by our daughter introducing us to Tom and Melinda. Tom and Melinda managed the church's First-Impressions Team, which we would become members of. They even opened their home to me while I was getting started at my new job, and we had never met or even moved yet.

Katie had graduated from Radford University and decided to stay where she was living. She received her master's degree at Radford as well. Now she works with children in need, in a neighboring county. She lives right down the road from us with her cat, Sasha.

Jacob is now a junior at a West Virginia college, where he plays on the men's volleyball team, and is an officer in the student government. He is majoring in sports management and wants to become a women's college volleyball coach after graduation. We had lost Jersey to age and illness, so Lilli is Jacob's emotional support dog now and loves being with him at college. Jacob's girlfriend, Tristan, attends a college nearby. She has become a significant part of our family. Beth Ann and I are sure that Jacob will not be moving back.

We had just moved to our current house so that we could be closer to our adult children, and I now must find my new normal, once again. I grew up as a city boy, but now we live in a part of the Blue Ridge Mountains called the New River Valley (NRV) in Virginia. I can no longer work a regular job because of my health. All my new doctors have come to a consensus and feel that it is not safe. So, I have had to leave my job as a Special Education Aide at a local high school. I had only been there for exactly one year to the day and made some wonderful friends that I know I will keep in touch with. During the past school year, I had to spend a lot of time at, or in, the hospital at one specialist or another's office, or at home, and that was just within a one-hundred-and-eighty-day school year. I have now been diagnosed with Parkinson's Disease as well as Stage Three kidney failure. Only because of my work ethic and love for the students I worked with, along with my family and God's grace and mercies, I made it through the year without losing any pay. It is hard to deal with the fact that I cannot work any longer. I was raised believing that the head of the household was supposed to take care of his family and be the breadwinner, no matter how many jobs he had to take on. I have had a job, even if it was just mowing lawns, since I was about ten years old. I can only think of two times in my fifty-plus years on this earth when I did not work.

I still have episodes of falling down, but my family, and even the dogs, know the signs of when I am about to hit the deck. They will run over to me and wrap me in a bear-hug and hold on to me, so that I do not fall. Then they ask me if I am okay, and when I come back around, they let go of me. The dogs will come up and nudge my leg to try and get me to sit down. I remember one time when Jacob was young, and I was just starting to have my falls. I had a really *hard* fall, and he was too little to catch me. He screamed out, "I am too young for this!" I felt so bad for him.

Now, I fill up my days with naps, watching TV, adhering to my med schedule, playing fetch with Marley, surfing the internet, or taking rides in "Lil' Red," my red Ford Ranger pick-up truck, with my furry sidekick and emotional support dog. She is a two-year-old Blue Merle Australian Shepherd. There is something about going for a drive in a truck, just a guy and his dog. Head out the window, ears flapping in the wind. (That would be Marley, not me. I would do it if I could, though.)

I do not really need to use an alarm anymore. I get up every morning with Beth Ann as she gets ready for work, or when my eyes open. I get greeted with a cold, wet nose and wagging, nubby tail (again, that would be Marley, not Beth Ann). I start my daily pharmaceutical dance, and get cleaned up, and then try to decide what to have for breakfast, after which, I feed Marley and let her out. I must make sure that when I get out of bed, I take it slow, or I might end up on the floor. When I take a shower, I must remember to not let it get too steamy. I cannot even be out in direct sunlight or any type of heat for any length of time. After a kiss and hug from my better half, Beth Ann, she must leave for work to start her thirtieth year as an elementary school teacher. In the past, I have been able to help her out with the lifting, moving, and setting up her room. This year, unfortunately, had its limits. My daily struggles are something that I would not wish on anyone, but I know that I am not the only one who has a lot on their plate.

When we are young, we think we are invincible. We did not worry about what we are doing to ourselves and that we are always right. I never thought that I would be in the shape I am currently in. However, I am also not surprised, knowing what I have put my body through in my short life. Luckly, I have learned lots of lessons and have done my best to put them into practice. The most important lesson is that Jesus went through far worse for my sins and the sins of others, so that we would know his love for us.

CHAPTER 39

I am not ready to become one of those guys who get up every morning and goes to the local coffee shop or fast-food restaurant to sit around and talk with other guys about the "good old days." I really do not think that I am old enough yet. On the other hand, if I did decide to do that, I have no doubt that my true-life stories would not be believed. I might end up giving one of the "old" guys a heart attack.

I have drafted my story down with a few revisions several times and have only shared it with people who know me; still, the reactions have always been the same.

They would say, "Wow, this is incredible; however, you are not telling us everything."

"We know there is more to the story."

The answer that I would always give was, "I've told you everything."

That was always a lie. No one knows the whole story but me and Jesus Christ. There are only two people who have come close. They are my wife, Beth Ann, and my best friend, Tommy.

Truthfully, the reason I have never told the whole story is that I am ashamed of parts of my life and how I lived it. I have always said that I am an open book, but that was just a cop-out to escape having to relive it or explain it. I *was* an open book. I just would pick which chapters people could read about. I wish I could apologize to all the people I have taken advantage of and hurt in the past. Yet, all I can do, now, is keep moving forward while continuing to listen to God's voice. Some things in this book could be considered big, while others are considered small; however, the pain and the shame are still the same.

CHAPTER 40

<u>Please let me pray for you:</u>

Heavenly Father, I come to You today with renewed hope. Hope that the words and messages You have allowed me to share in this book would be a Lamp, a Lifeboat, or a Ladder to the people who have read it while in the midst of their own darkness. I know that this is my life story, but let it be a way for others to find their own paths to You, our most gracious and loving Savior. I ask that You shower them all with Your grace and favor, just as You showered me with Your loving light when my life was at its darkest and I thought there was no hope. Bring people into their lives that will walk with them and not lead them astray. Equip them with the armor of God, to fight off all temptations and strife that would cause them to stumble as they come to know You better. I

humbly ask this in the name of the Son of the One True King, Jesus Christ. Amen

I want to truly thank you from the bottom of my heart for letting me take you on my road trip to redemption. I hope it brought you some insight on how God is always at work. You just have to trust in Him and be still.

The only thing I have left to share is my life verse:

Philippians 4:10-14 NIV

"I rejoiced greatly in the Lord that at last you renewed your concern for me. Indeed, you were concerned, but you had no opportunity to show it. I am not saying this because I am in need, for I have learned to be content, whatever the circumstances. I know what it is to be in need, and I know what it is to have plenty. I have learned the secret of being content in any and every situation, whether well-fed or hungry, whether living in plenty or in want. I can do all this through God who gives me strength. Yet, it was good of you to share in my troubles.

ABOUT THE AUTHOR

Christopher D. Craig, Sr., a compelling new author, shares with you his long-awaited autobiography. Craig, a native of Virginia, was born in Richmond, grew up in Chesterfield County, and has now settled, with his wife, Beth Ann, and his support animal, Marley, in the New River Valley. After realizing that "Life in the Fast Lane" wasn't part of his journey any longer, this former adrenaline junky, international cruise ship performer, and recording artist, takes you down the path he experienced to find the true meaning of **faith.** He found his faith in the midst of multiple serious health problems, some of which almost cost him his life. Christopher enjoys being with his family, attending church, and listening to and writing music. He also collects law enforcement patches and challenge coins, all while sharing the love and grace of the Lord. In conveying his testimony to others, he was encouraged to put it in book form. Christopher prays that, after reading his story, you will be encouraged to be a ***LAMP***, a ***LIFEBOAT***, or a ***LADDER*** to others.

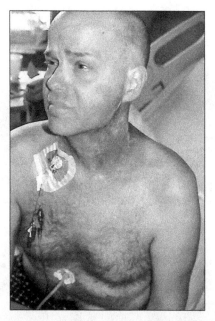

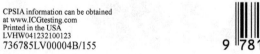

9 781662 865763